WHAT HAPPENED TO YOU?

"The first breath was wonderful."

"I got feelings of great happiness and relief from others in the delivery room."

"I was aware that my mother had great fear just at the birth experience."

"The feeling I had was of being all alone. I saw no one."

LIFE BEFORE LIFE

LIFE
BEFORE
LIFE

HELEN WAMBACH, PH. D.

BANTAM BOOKS
TORONTO · NEW YORK · LONDON · SYDNEY

LIFE BEFORE LIFE

A Bantam Book / March 1979
2nd printing .... July 1979
3rd printing .... March 1981

ISBN 0–553–20060–7

Published simultaneously in the United States and Canada

Bantam Books are published by Bantam Books, Inc. Its trademark, consisting of the words "Bantam Books" and the por-
trayal of a bantam, is Registered in U.S. Patent and Trademark
Office and in other countries. Marca Registrada. Bantam
Books, Inc., 666 Fifth Avenue, New York, New York 10103.

PRINTED IN THE UNITED STATES OF AMERICA

14 13 12 11 10 9 8 7 6 5

CONTENTS

LIFE
BEFORE
LIFE

In this time period I chose my sex because I was

INTRODUCTION

WHY I DID THIS RESEARCH

As word of my research spread, I was asked why I undertook the research.

"What got you interested in doing this?" The reporter commented that most psychologists stayed within the safe boundaries of the science without venturing into the unknown quicksands of the occult. Why, indeed, had I begun to ask such strange questions as "Are you choosing to be born?" and "Have you known your mother-to-be in a past life?"

I've always found this a difficult question to answer. I like to turn the inquiry aside with a joke by saying that after twelve years of teaching Introductory Psychology to college freshmen, I was bored. "If you think Psychology 101 is boring to study, you ought to try teaching it for years!" This is true enough. I never believed that behavior modification or learning theory provided a new insight into human behavior. As long as I received a paycheck for what I had done, I felt that was adequate proof of the theory that rewards and punishments do alter behavior. Beyond this initial insight, the works of Skinner and his associates elaborating on this theme were of little interest to me.

I became a psychologist because I felt it was a way to reach people and to learn about how the human mind worked. I found that psychological research didn't give me nearly as much information on how people thought and how they reacted as my work with patients in psychotherapy had taught me. For this reason I had laid research to one side as being something done by white-coated types, elaborating theories that were of decreasing interest. Subjects for research seemed to be largely white rats and college sophomores, because both these groups were easily available to researchers. I had learned all I cared to know about white rats and college sophomores.

When I began working with patients in psychotherapy, I grew much more absorbed in the fascinating ways that human beings deal with their problems. While I started out with the idea of the "doctor" seeing "patients," it didn't take me long to catch on that this was just a social idea and bore little relationship to what was actually happening in the consulting room when someone came to me in hopes of solving a human problem.

Of all the psychotherapy cases I have seen in the course of twenty years of therapy, I have never found two people the same. I have never found one explanation that would cover more than one case. The marvelous uniqueness of people and the complex ways in which they try to deal with their environment continued to fascinate me. The usual psychological theories seemed increasingly shallow to me. I wanted to tap deeper levels and explore aspects of personality that I recognized *did* exist—the spiritual dimension of man.

But my interest wasn't just professional. I'm a

human being too, and I have lived for fifty-three years in the tumultuous twentieth century. All of the common currents of our times—the shifting sands of national and international alignments, the fads and fancies of the American culture, the common trials of living in a rapidly changing technological society, are things I have shared with everyone else in America. Life kept happening to me, and not just to my "patients." And as the life of the twentieth century flowed through me, and as I flowed with the currents of the culture of my time and place, certain questions grew insistent. What are we here for? What is the purpose of all the emotions, struggles and anxieties of our times?

I remember the moment when my mother, eighty and senile, came out of her gentle fog of disorientation and asked, her eyes bright with fear, "I'm going to die, aren't I? Help me!" Like the readers of this book, I have had to face the wheel of life and the inevitable death of loved ones. My mother's life seemed to me to have opened like a flower in her childhood, and now that she was eighty and ready to leave this life, her mind and spirit were folding gently like a flower at the end of the day. Her mind wandered, as she confused her great-grandchildren with her childhood playmates. Her life was rounding gently to a close, and she was reliving experiences from the beginning of her eighty-year-old span. But through this gentle cloud of memories that was carrying her into death and beyond, at that one moment, her mind grew sharp and vivid with terror. She knew she was going to die, and she was afraid.

She had had a gentle life, secure in the cocoon of middle-class America. She had grown up a Methodist and had accepted the theology of her day with an unquestioning acceptance. In her way she had interpreted the Christian doctrine to mean that one must always demonstrate good manners toward others, go to church on Sundays, and trust in the authority of the minister and his expert reading of the Bible. But when the moment of full awareness of mortality struck through the fog of her mind, she was aware that this was not enough. What awaited her after death?

There was little I could do to reassure my mother. She asked that I read her the Bible, and I did that. I selected the passages that emphasized the immortality of the spirit, but I don't think she really heard me. Her bony old hand clasped mine tightly as I read the words of the Bible, but her eyes filmed over once again and she drifted gently back into her woolly thoughts. Four weeks later she drifted into a coma and left this life officially about three days after she had spoken her last words. She had gone gently into what she feared was a death of the soul.

But what *is* death? And if we must die, why are we born at all? It seems highly presumptuous of me to attempt to answer questions that have puzzled philosophers all through recorded history. But there were other questions that had formed my thoughts and now directed my research.

My mother's world was a secure and ordered one. Born in 1894, she had accepted all the technological inventions of her time as unqualified advances. She felt no discrepancy between her enjoyment of automobiles, radio, television, air travel, and the placid certitudes of her horse-and-buggy Protestant childhood. Progress would march hand in hand with literacy and enlightenment, and we would all move into a better world and grow richer and richer. She lived the American dream unquestioningly.

But I was of another generation. Born in 1925, I recalled the stark fear that the Great Depression brought to the faces of men on street corners. Though I was raised in pleasant circumstances, I was in the Midwest where the grimy reality of the Industrial Revolution spread its pall over the green countryside. In my youth I was to see that technology brought ugliness, division between men, and profound changes in the way in which we understood the world. Moving far away from the earth and conquering it had given us the power of gods to fly in the sky, to rain death and destruction on wide areas with our bombs and weapons. We had indeed become thunder gods, gods of miracles who could move mountains with our bulldozers. But when we moved those mountains we left the scars of open-pit mining. When we rained thunder from the skies like the volcano gods of old, we splintered human bodies and we lost our innocence.

World War II showed that it was not the gods that must be placated, but something inside the heart of man that allows him to destroy with savage intensity and on a grand scale those of his own kind who have offended him.

In the world of the simple farmer or tribesman, the doctrine of an eye-for-an-eye and a tooth-for-a-tooth was based on similar battles between animals for territorial power and a place in the pecking order. But when we humans had become gods ourselves and had harnessed the technological might of the atom bomb, the old tribal eye-for-an-eye grew too horrible to contemplate.

Anyone who has lived through the twentieth century and survived to 1978 is aware that man had brought something new in his world when he escaped the confines of his villages and the limitation of travel to the distance his legs could carry him. Tribal gods and an understanding of the universe based on simplistic notions of one group having more truth than another group, are luxuries that we cannot afford now that we have ourselves become gods. An understanding of our place in the universe and the true nature of our beings is forced upon us. For unless we grow, unless we reach that portion of our consciousness that reaches beyond the simple limitations of the human animal, we must either revert to our primitive surroundings through destroying our technological world, or indeed end our history as a species by making our world uninhabitable.

This hunger for a deeper understanding is very widespread in our culture. Some are trying to return to the certitudes of the old tribal religions, accepting unquestioningly doctrines laid down thousands of years ago. Their hope is that by returning to an earlier innocence and an earlier dependence upon the mysteries of an unknowable god, we can save ourselves from the consequences of our own acts. Others have seen that there is no return. We did become reasoning creatures who used our brain to understand the physical universe, and once we understood it, to change our physical universe. We did become gods in terms of the miracles we could bring about on earth. But now we must become gods in our profounder understanding of who we are, where we come from, and what our purpose must be.

And that, dear readers, is why I undertook this unusual bit of research. I didn't have the answers, though awareness was growing within me as it is with many in our culture of the worlds of consciousness beyond our physical awareness. I am a psychologist, and I know that there are depths of the mind that have remained untapped for most of us in our normal business of going about our affairs. I wanted to reach that portion of the mind of many people, and find out what insights might lie there, unrecognized and unreported. I knew that hypnosis was a way to move into the subconscious mind, into areas of consciousness normally blocked from our awareness. What answers lie there?

And so I began my exploration.

I

HOW I DID THE RESEARCH

The snow lay three feet deep around the Chicago motel where fifty-four people lay stretched out on blankets and pillows in the darkened banquet room. The great Chicago blizzard of January 1978 had kept some of these subjects from our earlier scheduled hypnosis sessions, but they were all finally able to get here, and now they lay on the floor waiting to explore their reason for being born.

As the lights dimmed and the room fell into darkness, it was so quiet I could hear the hum of the machinery that made our room a warm cave against the snowbanks outside the window. All fifty-four of my subjects had already been to two hypnotic trips to past lives in the past three hours, and I knew that 90 percent of them were experiencing past-life recall and responding to my hypnotic instructions. But as I sat in my chair and looked out over what seemed like a sea of bodies, I was once more amazed at this strange phenomenon. People who had never been hypnotized before, people who held varying beliefs about reincarnation, people who had traveled as far as 200 miles to experience this, were now all quietly waiting for my voice to take them on the most interesting journey of all—a journey into the origin of their current personality.

I began the hypnotic induction for the "birth trip" as I had done at least 400 times before. The words ran in my mind like a loop of tape, and I had learned how my thoughts could stray from what my voice was saying, and I heard my own voice come from a distance. I knew I was in an altered state of consciousness while I was conducting these sessions.

"Your eyes are closed and it feels good to close your eyes. The muscles of your face relax. The relaxation moves now from your facial muscles to your jaw muscles, and as your jaw muscles relax your tongue falls to the base of your mouth."

As I heard my voice say these familiar words, I once again wondered at the phenomenon that when the jaw muscles relaxed, people's thought seemed to become focused on my voice. When the jaw muscles relaxed, the voice box relaxed. As the speech centers relaxed, my subjects appeared to switch from the brain speech centers—the temporal lobe on the left side of the brain—into other areas of focus. They were moving into their right brains, where dreams, artistic endeavors, and scientific insight often seem to originate. I felt a pleasant, drifting feeling as I heard my voice continue the relaxation.

"The relaxation is moving now from your jaw muscles to your neck muscles, down to your shoulder muscles, down your arms to your elbows, down to your wrists, your hands and your fingers. Deeply and peacefully relaxed."

I felt my arms drop to a relaxed position on the arms of the chair as I followed my own instructions.

"The relaxation moves now from your shoulders

down your torso to your waist, and your breathing is easy and regular."

A familiar feeling of relaxation crept over me as my breathing changed on this instruction. My voice tone lowered, and became deeper and slower. My voice tones matched the deeper, slower breathing I was suggesting to my subjects.

"The relaxation is moving now from your waist to your hips, down your thighs to your knees, down your legs to your ankles, your feet and your toes. As I count to ten, your state of relaxation will deepen."

At this point in the hypnotic induction, I found myself sending comforting thoughts to my subjects mentally as I spoke these words. I felt uncomfortable if I ever forgot to send thoughts of well-being to all my subjects as I began to move them deeper into their own memories. Sometimes, at this point in the hypnotic induction, I would get a feeling that in a certain corner of the room someone was experiencing difficulty. I couldn't pinpoint exactly what this was, as I am not sure when I am experiencing telepathic communication from others. Like most of us, I require some kind of objective proof before I can accept telepathy as a fact. But still, I felt that in the right-hand corner of the room there was someone who was experiencing some anxiety. I sent a thought to this person that all would go well with them and that they could trust me. My voice droned on.

"One, deeper and deeper. Two, more and more relaxed. Three. Four. Five. Six. Seven. Eight. Nine. Ten."

I heard a cough from the right-hand corner of the room and wondered if this was the subject from whom I had received the telepathic message. I heard my voice say, "All discomfort will leave your awareness.

All of your muscles are relaxed." The coughing stopped. I proceeded.

"Your body is deeply relaxed now, but your mind is unusually alert and you have easy access to your memories. I want you to go back into your memory now, and find a snapshot of yourself that was taken between the ages of thirteen and eighteen. Focus on just one such snapshot.

"Now look closely at what you are wearing in that picture. You will go back in time now. You are now wearing that outfit of clothes. Do you like that outfit? How does it feel on your body?"

A snapshot quickly flashed in my own mind as I said those words. I saw myself as I was forty years ago, dressed in a crisp seersucker suit. I saw the youthful body I once knew and that had been buried for so many years under many different experiences and a changing body. But now that memory was alive within me, and I could feel my outfit on my body. I heard my voice continue.

"What shoes do you wear with that outfit?" In my mind I flashed on a pair of bobby oxfords, scuffed but comfortable. I smiled as I thought of all the different shoes that were being perceived and remembered by my fifty-four subjects lying on the floor. I wondered to myself about all the outfits being remembered which had been forgotten for so many years. I even had time to wonder what had happened to the fabric in those outfits of clothes. They receded somewhere in the past, mysteriously materializing when we wished to wear them, and then drifting through secondhand shops and then finally dying as dust rags or thrust into Goodwill bins. I had time to remember the data sheet on the birth experiences filled out by one of my subjects several weeks before, where she wrote: "I can only see my face in the picture, but I suddenly was back wearing the outfit I wore when that picture was taken. It all was vividly clear in my mind. I really can't understand this phenomenon of remembering under hypnosis, but it certainly is interesting!"

"Now I want you to go back into your memory and find a picture of yourself that was taken between the ages of six and twelve. Look closely at that picture. Where were you when that picture was taken? You will remember more and more details of that place where the picture was taken."

As my voice was saying these words, I found my-self back in my grandmother's yard in Iowa. I flashed on the memory of the old garage and the garden where the picture was taken. How many other gardens, how many other houses were being remembered in this instant of time among the fifty-five of us here in this room?

"You are back now in the fourth grade. You are sitting in your regular seat in the fourth grade. Are the windows on your left, or on your right? The teacher is in the front of the room. You want to ask her a question and her name flashes in your memory."

My teacher's name was Miss Forsberg; that lady had not crossed my memory for thirty-five years. Were the others also flashing on fourth-grade teachers long since forgotten?

"Now I want you to go back into your memory and find a picture of yourself that was taken between the ages of one and five. Look into the eyes of that child who is you. Do you remember being in that small a body? You are now three years old. You are sitting in a bathtub. Look down now and see your thighs, your knees, your legs, your ankles, your feet and your toes. How does it feel to be in this small a body? Become vividly aware of your body. You are three years old."

Many of my subjects reported that this was a pleasant part of the trip, as they found themselves splashing happily in bathtubs. My own response to these instructions was a sense of amazement at how light and active my body had been then. It was as though I could feel a much livelier metabolism than I knew now in my stout middle-age.

"Now I want you to line up all three snapshots. Yourself as a young child, yourself in middle-childhood, yourself as an adolescent. What is it that has stayed the same? Your body changed, your clothes changed, the background of the pictures changed. What is it that remains you? Are all these stages of childhood still somewhere in your mind?"

My thoughts were of the strange and profound puzzle of where the child we were exists in our here and now. Everything about us changes, often even our names. Where is the essential feeling of being "me" that continues through all of these physical changes? My voice droned on.

"I want you to recognize now that each of these snapshots represents just one twentieth of a second of the time you have been alive in this lifetime. Behind the picture of yourself as a young child, I want you to imagine a row of snapshots taken of all the other one-twentieths of a second that you were alive from birth to the age of five. See now that these snapshots would stretch to infinity. Behind the picture of yourself in middle-childhood, again a row of snapshots stretches with all the other one-twentieths of a second that you experienced in your growing-up years. And that row stretches to infinity. Behind the row of yourself as an adolescent, stretches the row of the other one-twentieths of a second that you lived through during that period of your life. If all the changes of your body as you matured sexually were recorded on film, if all the changes in your feelings about yourself, your ambitions, your dreams had been caught by a camera, they too would stretch to infinity.

"Look back now on these endless rows of snapshots that represent your past until the age of eighteen. How much of it do you remember? Almost all of it is lost to your conscious memory. The past you think you remember is a story told to you by your conscious ego, which remembers fragments and pieces from the past and threads them together to make a story called, 'My Past,' much as a film editor strings together snippets from film taken to make a movie. Recognize now that the past you think you remember is fragmentary and limited. For every moment in your past when you think you hated someone, you could find a moment when you loved that person. For every moment in your past where you felt guilt and shame, you could find a moment when you felt triumph and quiet self-satisfaction. Lost in those endless rows of snapshots of your growing-up years are potentials that you have never developed, feelings you have long since forgotten, options you have never realized. Recognize that now, at this moment, your past is nearly as changeable as your future. You may choose to remember parts of your past life, since forgotten, and you may choose to realize their potential in a future that is also yours to choose. This is what is meant by free will."

As my voice said these words, I tried to remember when I had consciously decided to put in this part of the hypnotic instructions. It simply came into my mind shortly after I began regressing people to the birth experience, and it felt good to me to say these things to my subjects. Apparently, the notion of showing people pictures of their past and helping them to understand the vast array of possibilities open to them was an idea that originated in my right brain, while I was also in a deeply relaxed state. By now I had learned not to question continually this kind of surprising but creative development. Along with my subjects, I have learned to get in touch with my right brain and to allow it sometimes the freedom to evolve new ideas and new approaches. Besides, I had realized that I knew very little about my own past, and even about the potentials that existed in me in childhood and early adolescence, that had been forgotten and put aside as I had made other choices of a life career. If this were true for me, surely it would be true for all the others who had come to me for this hypnotic session.

"Now your body is lying heavy on the floor, deeply relaxed. Your body is so heavy it feels as though it's sinking very gently into the floor. But your mind is free and light, floating, alert, yet deeply comfortable and relaxed. I want you to imagine, now, that you are a pinpoint of consciousness floating up away from your body and hovering near the ceiling of this room. You can perceive a dim light, and you're looking down now from a vantage point near the ceiling of this room. Can you see my body sitting in the chair here? My legs are crossed, my arms are resting on the arms of the chair. Now look and see if you can find your body on the floor. Can you see the others around you?"

This instruction was taken from my knowledge of the out-of-body experience reported by many subjects and from my own dream states. My subjects reported it to be a pleasant feeling, so I felt it was a good introduction to moving into deeper states. I continued with this guided fantasy portion of the trip.

"Now you are floating out, insubstantial as smoke, through the roof of this building and out into the clear night sky. The stars are sparkling bright and the moon is out, and below you the city lies covered with snow. You are floating higher and higher, up into the velvety blackness of space. You feel marvelously light and free as you soar up and away."

I knew from experience that some of my subjects would fall into what is called sleep at this point, but I felt it was very important to get my subjects as deep into the state of hypnosis as possible before I asked the questions on the birth experience. I found that many subjects could not get the answers to my questions unless they were very deeply hypnotized, so I began another phase of the hypnotic induction to bring them to this deep state.

"Your conscious mind will not understand what I am about to say next. I am speaking to your subconscious mind. I want you to reduce your brain-wave electrical potentials down to five cycles per second. Your brain wave amplitude readings will be five cycles per second. At this deep, slow-wave state, you will be able to reach the deeper portions of yourself where the answers to my questions will come. As I count to five, your brain wave activity will slow to a rhythmical five cycles per second. One, deeper and deeper. Two, more and more relaxed. Three. Four. Five."

I chose the instruction to move to a brain wave amplitude of five cycles per second based on some data some friends of mine had gathered. They reported that when their subjects were hooked to biofeedback machines, and were registering between zero and four cycles per second, they were unable to recall when they awoke what they had said. They had been "asleep." But when they were questioned when in this deep state, they often reported mystical insights. It seemed that in this deep state material could be reached that was not normally available to the conscious mind. How many of us have awakened in the middle of the night with some great insight, only to drift back to sleep and forget.

As I wanted my subjects to stay awake just enough to remember their responses, I chose five cycles per second as the ideal state for receiving information on the pre-birth experience. As yet this biofeedback work has not been published or confirmed. I hope to do much more work in this area so we can begin to relate specific EEG recordings with subjective phenomena experienced when the subject is in that particular brain-wave state. I had found that this instruction did result in apparently deeper hypnotic trance, and therefore, tended to increase the response of my subjects to my questions on this birth trip.

"I want you to go now to the time just before you were born into your current lifetime. Are you choosing to be born?"

I allow just five seconds for my subjects to respond to this question. I have found that the more time I allow for answers to flash in the mind, the more the conscious ego interferes. When the answers flash rapidly, apparently they seem to be coming from the right brain, or subconscious. When answers are slow in coming, the conscious mind tends to speculate on the "right answer" and to deal with the concept on a rational basis. I was looking for material from the subconscious, so I gave my subjects very little time to respond to my questions.

"Does anyone help you choose? If anyone helps you choose, what is your relationship to the counselor?"

I asked this question because in my initial experiments with the pre-birth experience I had been surprised at the reported presence of others during the decision-making time before birth. I was curious as to how my subjects would identify these helpers, so I included this question in my survey.

"How do you feel about the prospect of living this coming lifetime?"

I found that I had to phrase this question very carefully. If I asked how they felt about being born, I would get responses relating to physical fears of emerging from the birth canal. So I had sharpened the question so that the answer would be related to the feelings about the lifetime rather than the birth process.

"Are you choosing the last half of the twentieth century to experience physical life for a reason? What is that reason?

"Have you chosen your sex for this coming lifetime? If you have, why have you chosen to focus as a man or as a woman in this lifetime?

"What is your purpose for coming into this, your current lifetime?"

I knew from past experiences that this was the question most of my subjects wished to have answered in this hypnotic session. Many of them were looking for their reason for being alive, and it had directed their search through books, study and experience in altered states of consciousness. Would they find it tonight? I knew from my own responses while hypnotized that this is the hardest question of all to answer. In my own case, I flashed on the answer that I had had three major purposes, two of which I had managed to meet already and one which still lay ahead of me. But the exact nature of that third purpose of mine remained vague. I wondered if any of my subjects here tonight would find their reason for being alive.

"Now I want you to direct your attention to your mother-to-be. Have you known her in a past life? If you have known her, what was your relationship before?

"Now, direct your attention to your father-to-be. Have you known him in a past life? If so, what was your relationship to him before?

"Are you aware now, before you are born, of others that you will know in the coming lifetime? Have you known them in past lifetimes? Do you know what role they will play in your coming life? Will you know them as lovers, or mates? Will you know them as children or other relatives? Will you know them as friends?"

I left more time between my questions in this section of the hypnotic regression. Many of my subjects flashed answers to these questions rapidly, but a good deal of material was there to explore. So I allowed about a minute between each of the questions about relationships in the current life, and how they had been known in past lives.

"Now I want you to direct your attention to the developing fetus who will be you. Are you experiencing *inside* the fetus? *Outside* the fetus? In and out? When does your consciousness fully join that of the fetus?"

This is one of the most interesting questions in my series. I knew from past experience that it was important to phrase the question as carefully as possible. I asked first if they were experiencing inside the fetus, because there is a tendency for people to choose the first possible response, and I didn't want to prejudice my data against the common notion that life begins at conception. But I had found from my initial work with the hypnotic birth experience that many people experienced being in and out of the fetus, so it was important to put in that possibility in my questions.

"Are you aware of the attitudes and feelings of your mother just prior to your birth?"

I had added this question because I was curious about the emotional relationship of the fetal personality and the mother's personality. Do children know the feelings of their mothers?

"Now you are moving down the birth canal. You will have no pain, but you will be aware of sensations. Now you are moving down the birth canal. What are you experiencing now?"

I found it was important to suggest away pain because I had found that people in deep trance state physically moved and experienced pain in this part of the birth experience unless I told them they would not feel the pain. I had had subjects waking up with severe muscle cramps, painful headaches, and other signs of trauma experienced during the birth reflected in their current body responses. By telling my subjects they would not experience the pain, I had found I could eliminate most of these negative responses.

"Now you have emerged from the birth canal. You've been born. What are you experiencing now?"

I used the word "experiencing" rather than asking for specific sensations, because I didn't want to prejudice my subjects' responses. I didn't want to suggest anything about lights or cold.

"Are you aware of the attitudes and feelings of others in the delivery room after your birth?"

I wanted to know whether my subjects were responding as newborn infants, or whether they remained in full awareness of the delivery room even though they could not physically see it or respond to it. I knew of many instances where subjects who had had surgery were able to recall under hypnosis the happenings in the operating room when they were supposedly "out" under anesthesia, and I wondered if this would be true with the newborn infant.

"Now you are leaving that place. You are floating up and away from the delivery room. You are floating back up into space, back up to your cloud. As you climb onto your cloud, and stretch out and relax, all awareness of pain and discomfort leaves you. As you float on your cloud, and as I count, all your body systems will return to normal. You will have no physical or emotional discomfort as a result of your experiences on this trip. You are now floating up and away from that place where you were born. Your body is relaxing and all your organ systems are returning to normal."

I had found it was very important to include this instruction. Even in spite of this instruction, my subjects often reported feelings of sadness, and even some residual instances of pain such as headache. So I strongly emphasized the removal of pain. I found this to be necessary in the birth experience trip, and much less necessary in past-life recall. For some reason I don't understand, experiencing the pre-birth and birth is more disturbing to people than recalling their past lives.

"Now you are floating on your cloud, and I'm taking you deeper. As I count you will become more and more peaceful and serene. Your mind is floating free, and you have a feeling of peace and harmony around you. One, deeper and deeper. Two, more and more relaxed. Three. Four. Five. You are floating on your cloud now, and there's a beautiful white light all around you. The light is very pure and intense, and it's growing brighter. There's a tightly budded rose in your solar plexis. Rays of energy from the light gently unfurl the petals of the rose until the heart of the rose is exposed. Dancing rays of energy from the light flood into the heart of the rose, and through the rose move through your solar plexis. The energy waves from the light wipe away any negative after-effects from your experience on this trip. The waves of light energy bring a lightness, peace and serenity to your mind and your body."

This image had come to me while I was hypnotizing several years ago. I was not aware until after I had said it that it was a version of the old Tibetan mantra, "Om mani padmi hum." This mantra, translated, means "May the petals of the lotus open." The Kundalini yoga system teaches that the solar plexis "chakra," or energy center, controls the emotions. So in essence what I was doing by moving the light through the rose into the solar plexis was bringing the energy of the universe in to harmonize any disturbances in the solar plexis chakra. I am not particularly a believer in Kundalini yoga, or any Indian system, but my subjects find this a soothing image and I like it, too. Perhaps the idea of this image was placed in my mind by some ancient yogi somewhere who is kibitzing on my hypnosis sessions! At any rate, I'm an American, so if it works I use it.

"Now it is time to return to the here and now. When you awaken, the answers that flashed in your mind to my questions will be vivid in your memory. They will remain vivid for months and you will be able to recall them whenever you wish. When I hand out the data sheet, the answers that came to you will flood back into your memory and you will be able to fill out the data sheet without difficulty.

"Now, picture to yourself a ball of golden energy sparkling out in a far corner of space. Picture that energy rolling and flowing down through the darkness of space, penetrating the atmospheric envelope of earth, coming down to the Western Hemisphere, coming down to this room and entering the crown of your head. As the energy enters the crown of your head, a sense of well-being sweeps through you, and all your bodily energies are restored. You are in a very good humor when you wake up, and you feel great. One, the ball of energy is moving now into the crown of your head and into your face. Two, the ball of energy is moving now into your jaw muscles and into your neck. Three, the energy is moving into your shoulders. Four, the energy is moving down your arms to your elbows, down to your wrists, your hands and your fingers. Five, the energy is moving from your shoulders down your torso to your waist. Six, the energy is moving into your hips. Seven, the energy is flowing down your thighs to your knees. Eight, the energy is moving down your legs, your ankles, your feet and your toes. Nine, your body is alive now with vibrant energy and you're ready to wake up, feeling refreshed, feeling great. Ten, open your eyes—you're awake."

I knew from experience that the group would be slow to move after this third hypnotic session. My subjects became so relaxed with three sessions in a row that they didn't move, but just smiled pleasantly at me when I woke them up.

What would be the reactions of these subjects? The best part of the sessions, for me, is hearing the stories my subjects report after they awaken.

This was my last data-collection session. I had come to the Midwest to find out whether Midwestern subjects reported different answers to these questions than my subjects in California. There was no way I could find any proof or verification for the answers reported by my subjects. I was running a kind of Gallup Poll of hypnotized subjects. But I reasoned that if cultural beliefs were responsible for the answers I was getting, perhaps subjects in a different part of the country would respond differently to the questions. This would tend to prove that the answers were based on common cultural beliefs, rather than coming from a deep part of the subconscious mind.

II

MY CHICAGO GROUP
REPORTS
THEIR EXPERIENCES

I switched on the lights and looked around the room. My subjects were stretching and slowly sitting up. They had that sleepy, rather spaced-out look I had come to recognize was the result of spending four hours on the floor exploring their own right brains. As I passed out the data sheets, many of my subjects smiled at me. They seemed in a remarkably pleasant mood, but very thoughtful and quiet. Several of them told me they had tears in their eyes, though they didn't feel sad. One woman told me as I handed her the data sheet, "Oh, I felt such compassion for that baby who was me. I felt such sadness to leave the place where I was to come back into physical life. It seemed so hard to be confined in a little body, and to lose the lightness and the love I had known in the between-life state." She laughed as she showed me the tears that were rolling down her cheeks.

I reassured her that hers was a common reaction, and that soon she'd feel cheerful. "Oh, I feel cheerful enough," she said, "it's just that I realize that birth is not a joyous occasion. The two deaths I had in the two past lives tonight were very pleasant experiences. It's getting born that seems the tragedy."

I noticed that nearly half the group did not write on their sheets. I asked how many of them had gone too deep on this trip, and about 40 percent of the group acknowledged that they had not recalled anything from the time I had counted down to five after asking them to see the pictures of themselves in childhood. About ten of them had gone too deep and did not hear my instructions about the pictures. Another fourteen reported that no answers to my questions came to them, though they seemed deeply relaxed. Two subjects reported that they were wide awake the whole time and were not hypnotized on this trip. Neither of these subjects had responded earlier to the hypnotic trips, so I assumed that they were quite resistant to the hypnotic process.

These findings were typical of my experimental groups everywhere. Just under 50 percent of my subjects did report getting the answers to my questions on the birth experience. When I was selecting the cases for my statistical analysis, I puzzled over this phenomenon. Ninety percent of my subjects had gotten the past-life recall; what was there about the birth experience that was so difficult? Of course, it could have been the fear of the actual birth-canal experience that was inhibiting my subjects. On the other hand, this wouldn't affect their responses to the questions about choosing to be born. I reasoned that if they were fantasizing about past lives, certainly they could fantasize about being born. At least they know for sure that they're here now. Perhaps only some of us are able to reach this level that has been called the super-conscious. Perhaps also my instruction to go to five cycles per second meant that I was sending many of my subjects so deep that they could not recall later what they did experience on the birth trip.

By this time I had accumulated enough data sheets to know that I would probably get only about 40 percent usable data sheets from any given group. Because I wanted the answers to these questions to come from a deep level, I eliminated all data sheets where my subjects had written such things as "I think I was awake the whole time, and just thought of these answers." I also eliminated any subjects who had read my article in *New Realities* magazine on the birth experience, because their conscious minds might have selected the answers to the questions based on knowing my findings to date.

I had combed the literature for references to the pre-birth experience in the occult tradition, but had found little that would suggest a set of responses my subjects would consciously know. The experience after death has been described in Raymond Moody's book, *Life After Life,* so that some of my subjects on the past life trips may have been reporting a death experience similar to what they had read. But except for the idea that we are born with other groups of people in order to work out karma—an idea not just from the Eastern occult tradition, but in the Edgar Cayce books as well—I have found no references to who helps us choose, or whether or not we are aware of our purposes before we are born.

My subjects gathered up their blankets and pillows and walked slowly out of the room. Some of them were smiling, while others looked very serious. Nearly all of my subjects thanked me for the experience. This always surprised me, since I feel I should thank them for being subjects in my research. One by one, they handed me their filled-out data sheets.

As I read the data sheets filled out by my subjects, I found that they were very typical of my groups not just in the Midwest, but in California too. The first sheet that I read was that of a young man who reported as follows:

"Yes, I chose to be born. Someone did help me choose and it seemed to be some voice that I trusted greatly. It was kind, helpful and wise, very wise. My feelings about the prospect of being born were very positive. When you asked the purpose for this lifetime, it flashed that I was to broaden people's minds.

"I chose this time period to be born because it is a great period of change where people need stability within themselves. I am supposed to help them somehow. I did choose to become a male, because it is good for my work, and I enjoy that sex role. My mother was my wife in a past life, my father was my son. I got some faint flashes of mates or lovers, but nothing clear.

"As to children and other relatives, I felt uncertain except for one uncle who came through clearly as someone I knew before. I did have many friends from past lives. I attached to the fetus when I decided to meet it in the womb of my mother just before birth. The feelings of my mother were very positive and loving and warm. When you asked for the birth experience, I felt odd, tingling sensations around a fleshy ball that was me. My impression after birth was one of happiness and the doctor seemed pleased and my mother was very happy.

"I feel that this lifetime feels very good and positive for me and I feel a burst of energy and a purpose after this session."

The next data sheet read:

"Yes, I chose to be born, and some kind of teacher seemed to be consulting with me about it. I was eager to be born. But when asked a purpose for this lifetime, all I got was to wait for something, and I don't know what. I didn't seem to know why I was in this time period, but I did know I chose to be a female this time because I had been a male in my most previous life. It seemed I didn't know my mother or my father from past lives, but I did know my husband and several friends from past lives.

"I was attached to the fetus only when I was ready to be born. I was aware that my mother had great fear just at the birth experience. When I was in the birth canal, all I felt was a spinning and sinking feeling. After I was born, I saw a white room with brown wooden furniture. That was all I was aware of.

"This hypnotic trip was a strange experience. I chose this life amidst some kind of assemblage. I had a few choices but they were not unlimited."

A young man dropped off his data sheet at the table and smiled ruefully. "This was a weird trip. I had a sense of compulsion when you asked if I chose to be born, but I didn't get the answers to any of the other questions until I was in the birth canal. This was really strange!"

His data sheet read:

"I don't think I chose to be born, I have the feeling I must have been told. When you asked me about living another lifetime, I experienced a crushing feeling in my body. When you asked the purpose, the only thing that flashed was that I had to experience this life, though I had no choice in the matter. The birth canal experience was again that feeling of crushing with a heavy sensation in my chest. Immediately after birth I did get strong impressions. I gasped for breath and felt more at ease. All I was aware of was that I was so relieved that the crushing feeling had left me."

The next data sheet I picked up was someone who did choose to be born, and in answer to the question: "Did anyone help you choose?" the answer was:

"Yes, one of us. (Perhaps "us" expresses it best. It was a group of some kind and we were coming together.)

"When you asked about the prospect of being born, I felt I would have preferred more rest and preparation but it was time to begin. When you asked the purpose, it was to serve the evolution of mankind's will. I chose this time period because it is also personally appropriate, because of the path of karmic ties that was involved in this lifetime. I did choose my sex in order to experience my relationships with others in a different framework. I knew my mother and father from past lives, as well as my husband and friends, but not my children.

"When you asked about the attachment to the fetus, I felt that I didn't really attach until my mother was in labor. The birth-canal experience was interesting. I felt a fusion of my energy coalescing, but I felt anger at the loss of control as soon as I was born. I was not ready for the emotions of others I was experiencing once I was born."

The next data sheet also expressed the subject's resentment at having to enter this, her current lifetime.

"No, I didn't choose to be born, but a present sister of mine seemed to be there urging me to be born. I did not want to because I didn't feel I was ready. I knew that one of my purposes for this lifetime was to learn to accept my father as the person he is and yet to get to know my mother better who was my best friend in a previous life. Both of them would be alive at this time, which is why I chose this time period.

"I also chose my sex because I was a male in the

previous life where I knew my father. My mother had been a dear friend in the same lifetime where my father had whipped me in his role as a jailor. I got no impression of mates or lovers being related to me in past lives, but it was clear to me that my younger brother had the same relationship to me in a past lifetime. I wasn't aware of when I was attached to the fetus, but I do know that my mother was lonely, but happy to be carrying me.

"The birth-canal experience was very hard and lasted a very long time, even though it was just a few seconds here in the hypnosis. My impressions after birth were that the woman who assisted my mother was very tired and my mother was happy that I was a girl. My feelings after birth were I felt I fought the purpose of this life, because I didn't want to come at that time, due to my father and no one else.

"This experience has provided me with some insight into my true feelings. Thank you."

The next data sheet I looked at from the Chicago group was scribbled and hard to read. I noted that this subject reported that she was experiencing automatic writing. I did tell my subjects that their subconscious would report their experiences even though they would not be consciously aware of it, and this data sheet was an example of the subconscious bursting through the restraints of the conscious mind and producing answers from the deeper levels. The data sheet reported:

"Yes, I chose to be born and yes, a series of faces seemed to be around me. Many faces—the first was distinctly male. My feelings about the prospect of being born were that being born is a testing of fulfillment. Something one must do. The purpose was to behold, to see. I chose this time period to be part of becoming, to be part of something which will develop in this time period. I chose my sex because I was going to have children who would be people I knew in past lives. I knew my mother before, but not my father; I knew my husband in a past life and I knew my children and friends. I was not attached to the fetus until the first breath and expulsion from the womb.

"My mother was unhappy. Her life was not what she would have it. I was aware of her unhappiness. In the birth-canal experience I had a backache and then flexed and felt better. The impressions after birth were that it was very funny because people think you know nothing, but you know it all, and it's very funny."

The next data sheet again showed a reluctance to be born, but an agreement in the end.

"I eventually chose to be born, and I was convinced by a careful chiding shortly before birth. Before birth I was involved in immense discussions about why I should or should not go. I felt ambivalence about the prospect of living this lifetime, and a strong feeling of duty and responsibility. When you asked about the purpose of this lifetime, I flashed on an exact answer which was, 'To be like an arrow in the center of the ring target. To be beautiful, to be made beautiful.'

"When you asked about the time period, the twentieth century, it flashed in my mind that the electromagnetic conditions were right for me. I chose to be a woman to lessen the shock of physical sensations. When you asked about the karmic ties, I flashed on answers to all. I seemed to have known all the people in my life, or most of them, in past lives. When you asked about attachment to the fetus, I felt that I delayed and just barely made it in as the contractions started. I was aware of the sensations of my mother when I was in the birth canal.

"My impressions after birth were of a painful blurring of the spirit and body. I seemed to lose awareness of other people's feelings and of the knowledge I had once I was born."

The next report also was of someone who resisted the process of living another lifetime.

"I didn't choose to be born, and I thought when you asked that question, 'Oh, no, not again—I'm so comfortable here.' (Wherever here might be!) I did have help in choosing. Two counselors showed me how my mother would want me, and my mother-to-be wanted me so much. She would guard and love me so it would all be okay. I felt they were reassuring me. My feeling about the prospect of being born was I felt I had served well in my last life and I wanted a rest, and felt it was too soon to return, because it would be rather traumatic.

"When you asked about purposes for this lifetime, I felt that I am here to make people happy in an everyday sense. The purpose came through not to be super-religious or anything, but just to create a sense of happiness in the people I would be with. When you asked about choosing the time period to be born, I sensed troubled times and the last of a kind of era. I knew it would be rough and that's one reason I hesitated to be born. When you asked about choosing the sex, I flashed immediately I had chosen to be a woman because it is easier to make people happy by being female. I did know my mother from a past life, but my father seemed very vague. My husband I knew in a past life, but I didn't know my children. One friend came through as someone I'd known well in a past life. I was aware before my birth that my mother was very happy and wanted me so much. Knowing that gave me courage to come.

"I got no impression as to when I was attached to

the fetus. My impression after birth was of extreme cold and a feeling of 'Now what?'

"I am puzzled by my vague purpose. But it seemed when I was under hypnosis that it was clearly to devote myself to other people and not to myself."

The next data sheet was interesting because the subject, a male, had preferred to be female. This subject reported:

"Yes, I chose to be born, and a guide or teacher counseled me. It was a big decision and involved a lot of thought and debate with my guide. My purpose for this lifetime was to become free of materialism and to combat negativeness, to combine male and female emotions for control, love and strength.

"I chose this time period because I and my guide felt that this would be harder, but best for me. I wanted to be a female for pleasure, but I chose male because, again, for me, the test would be harder. I did know my mother and my father in a past life, together with my wife. I didn't get any impression as to whether or not I knew my friends before. I seemed to attach to the fetus, or at least become aware of it right after conception.

"I was aware of the feelings of my mother, and a strange feeling came through. I felt tied to her as a possible enemy, because my relationship with her in a past life had not been good. She seemed to be aware of this.

"There was no problem with the birth-canal experience and my impressions after birth were pleasant."

The next subject, again a man, chose his sex for a different reason. He reported:

"Yes, I chose to be born, but a high council seemed to be helping me make the decision. I was excited at the prospect of living in this lifetime and felt that my purpose was to help others. When you asked about the twentieth century, it flashed in my mind that this was the era of outer space, and that was why it was important for me, but I don't know why that should have come to my mind.

"I did choose my sex because the male is dominant and, apparently, I needed that in this lifetime. I did not know my mother from a past life, but my father was in a lifetime in Egypt with me. I also seemed to know some friends who were people I commanded at some past time period. I attached to the fetus only after it was fully formed, just before birth. I did feel warmth from my mother's body, and her fear of the birth while I was in the womb.

"The birth-canal experience was one of no pain, but a sliding feeling, with a light at the end of the tunnel. My impression after birth was that my skin was blue and I was very, very cold. The doctor was laughing."

The next subject again chose to be born as a duty, not a pleasure.

"My brother and some soul guardian seemed to be helping me. When you asked about the prospects of being born, I felt, 'Oh, no, not again,' but I also knew I had to learn more. My purpose for this lifetime seemed to be to develop my psychic abilities and correct my diet and health and mental and emotional attitudes. I chose this time period to reexperience life with my present family and friends, whom I had known before and who would be alive in this time. I chose to be a woman to experience motherhood in this life.

"I knew my mother before as a sister in one past life, and my father as a father in a past life. I knew my husband, my children, and friends.

"My attachment to the fetus was kind of off and on; it wasn't clear to me when I was actually a part of the fetus. I was aware that my mother hoped for a son to replace one she had lost. The birth-canal experience was very tight, but warm, and after birth I felt a kind of sterility, and a loudness and a brightness, and I felt that the outer world was so unresponsive. I seemed to feel that my 'soul' retained the knowledge that I had attained throughout previous lives after birth."

The next data sheet was handed to me by a quiet young man who had spoken little about his past-life trips. I was curious about his experiences on the hypnotic trip and read it eagerly. I noticed that he was one of my subjects who seemed to go quite deep, and I was afraid he had gone too deep to get the birth experience, but I was wrong.

"I think I was reluctantly talked into being born. A wise man whom I respected, obeyed and loved helped convince me it would be good for me to be born now. He was a gentle, kind, but firm man. My feelings about the prospect of living the coming lifetime were that I was sort of scared, but I knew that my purpose was somehow to help. Apparently, I chose the twentieth century for the people that I would be with. I didn't get any impression of choosing my sex. I'm just not sure about that. I seemed to know my mother before, but it didn't come through very vividly. My father, though, I definitely knew from a past life where we had been close. I knew one of my children from a past life.

"I seemed to become aware of the fetus when Mom was five or six months along. I knew that my mother was nervous and feeling a little sorry for herself. During the birth-canal experience, I feel that it mashed my face and my arms down. Immediately after birth I was cold and the room was cold. It pissed me off to be cold and held away from Mother in the lights. I was aware of everything going on around me in the delivery room. Daddy was awed and worried, but moved and quiet. Mother was nervous and talky, then groggy. The doctor was nonchalant but kind."

The next data sheet was interesting because of the additional comments the subject had written.

"The feelings of being born seemed very real. It appeared that I was an observer to the first forming of the fetus, but I also felt I was experiencing what the fetus was, sort of future-traveling instead of past-traveling. I did choose to be born, I think, but I was with a group of loved ones who supported me and encouraged me to go through this coming lifetime. But I wanted to stay with the loved ones, and not be born on earth again. I did know that one of my purposes was to love, but I got no impression for why I had chosen this time period. I felt that I have always been female and that I didn't really choose it, it just seemed the most natural thing.

"I knew my mother in a past life when she was my sister. I didn't know my father before, or my husband, but I did know my children from past lives. I wasn't aware of the feelings of my mother, and the only experience I had in the birth canal was that it was very wet and warm. The impressions after birth were of cold and sensations. (Touch especially; there were others touching me, and they felt cold.) Other people in the delivery room seemed so busy—just so much activity compared to the womb."

The next data sheet returned to me was from someone who seemed quite reluctant to be born.

"No, I didn't choose to be born, I was instructed to return. It seemed to me that I just followed instructions (don't know who was instructing). I felt no rebellion, just that it was not really my choosing. I was quite apprehensive about living the coming lifetime. One of the purposes for this lifetime seemed to be to teach and to minister to mankind and to work on the development of the greater use of the mind to ultimately teach.

"I chose this time period because somehow the psychology field flashed into my mind, and I felt that psychology was moving too slowly and hampering the spiritual development of mankind. I didn't seem to have chosen my sex. My mother had been my sister in a past life where we fought all the time. My father had been my grandfather in another lifetime. My husband was a Sioux Indian when I was a French padre, and I didn't like him then either! I seemed to have an attachment to the fetus from the inception, but this is vague. My mother was very happy. In the birth-canal experience, I started to hold my breath and then breathe very heavily.

"After birth, I was mostly aware of being happy to be in a wanted situation. This has been a very enlightening hypnotic experience as I have had the feeling since my earliest memories that I was here for a reason, and have had some interesting mental talents develop."

The next data sheet reported reluctance to be born, but eventual agreement.

"There was a council of twelve who helped me choose, and I did choose freely. But I was not eager to begin this life cycle. I felt that the purpose of this lifetime was to bring some special education and knowledge to the world to set up a special council on the earth's plane. I chose this time period because it would be favorable for establishing such a council.

"I chose my sex in this life so that I could have specific experiences, and have enough material substance to continue the work. I didn't know my mother in a past life, but I did know my father, and my husbands. I attached to the fetus just the day before birth. My mother felt sad and had much fear. My birth-canal experience was peaceful, and my feelings after birth were that I was floating and then suddenly I had a sharp awareness. I heard a voice say, 'What a beautiful little one.'

"I felt my father was also part of the inner council of which I was a part. It feels as if I have a very heavy position to carry through in this life."

As I gathered the data sheets and put them in my briefcase, I felt eager to return to my office in California and total up all the answers. By now I knew what many of them would be, but the time had come to publish my report and share it with others.

And so, now for the answers that came from 750 hypnotized subjects.

III

CHOOSING TO LIVE AGAIN

All of us will agree, I think, that life can indeed be difficult and unpleasant at times. Yet we cling to life and fear death. Modern medicine devotes itself to the preservation of life. It is our most sacred value in our secular culture. Disasters are measured by how many lives are lost, not by the amount of pain and suffering endured by the survivors. The fear of death is strong in many of us, and is the motive power behind our phobias. Some would say that the fear of death lies behind all the religions of the world, and because we wish to remove the fear of death from our minds, we invent heaven, hell, reincarnation.

But is it death we fear, or is it the pain, physical and mental, that we expect to experience just before death? "He went fast, a heart attack in his sleep. Mercifully, he was spared the physical pain of a long illness." We've all thought that, when we heard of a friend's sudden death.

Is the fear of death also the fear of the unknown? Is it a kind of separation anxiety that we feel when we face a new experience? Shakespeare's Hamlet felt that:

"To sleep, perchance to dream. But in that sleep of death, what dreams may come?"

The birth experience under hypnosis, in my workshop format, followed three death experiences in three previous lives. All subjects were given the option to skip the death experience if they wished. Interestingly, less than 10 percent of subjects chose the option to avoid their death in past lives. Of this 10 percent of subjects only 2 percent avoided the death in all three past life trips.

Admittedly, it's one thing to "fantasize" or "remember" past deaths and another thing to actually experience death. I made no claims that experiencing "past life recall" in my hypnotic workshops was therapeutic in any way. Yet many subjects told me that they had lost their fear of death after the workshop experience.

"You know, I felt I was making up my past lives in your workshop. Didn't think it was real. But a couple of days later, I realized that something had happened; something important to me," Nancy told me. We'd met at a friend's house a month after Nancy had been in my workshop. "I used to be terrified of going under anesthesia, even for pulling a tooth. I fought the idea of being unconscious. I thought it was like death and I was plain scared. But after 'imagining' my death in a past life, I'm not afraid of death, or of being unconscious."

So I knew that 90 percent of my subjects found that death was pleasant. Yet none of them reported that they had lost their zest for life. So I thought that they would find the return to life in another body a basically pleasant process.

I was wrong.

Of the 750 subjects reporting the birth experience, 81 percent said that they did choose to be born and that it was their choice to make. But I found that perhaps I was asking the wrong question. While a majority chose to be born, many did so quite reluctantly only after consulting with advisers. My subjects reported that while they had the right to refuse to go through a planned lifetime, they felt a duty to do so. It was rather like freely choosing to do service in the army; not something one would automatically do, but something that was necessary and so reluctantly agreed to. But there are many different impressions of my subjects, even among those who chose to be born.

Only 28 percent of my subjects felt enthusiastic about being alive again and felt that they had planned carefully and were ready to begin.

"I chose to be born and I felt that I was helped to choose because I needed to continue and correct the work of my last life. I was eager for the experience of this life." (Case A-157)

"Yes, I chose to be born, and there were helpful energies all around me, but I made the final decision. I didn't feel any apprehension." (Case A-176)

"I did choose to be born, and I had others helping me choose. I had the choice of several entities [Fetal bodies]. The choice was a natural one, because I knew them all—those I would be living with. I was looking forward to this lifetime with great anticipation. I was worried, though, about the health of my mother and considered not making it." (Case A-217)

"Yes, I chose to be born and many were advising me. I was looking forward to seeing those who had already gone ahead of me." (Case A-220)

"Yes, I chose to be born. I was excited, happy, confident. Helping me choose was a group who chose to come together. We each had guidance and specific work to do. I was excited about the prospect of being born and I knew I could do it right." (Case A-393)

"Yes, I chose to be born and a small group helped me choose. We were about six people in the group. My feelings about the prospect of the coming lifetime was a feeling of excitement because I was to participate in exciting changes that were going to happen on earth. When I chose to be born, I knew I would be meeting up with the people I was with in the future. Some would help guide me." (Case A-372)

"Yes, I chose to be born. I had a very strong sensation of flowing from my expanded, dispersed self down into my physical center, and had a vision of it. I think someone helped me choose, but if they did, it was prior to the space I experienced, because I felt my own pressure to enter physical reality. My feelings about the prospect of being born were very positive and I was impatient to begin." (Case A-349)

"Yes, I chose to be born, and there were others around me giving me advice and counsel about the coming lifetime. I felt ready for the coming life, but I would have liked to stay in the other energy. But when I did enter the fetus I felt joy to be born." (Case A-345)

"Yes, I chose to be born, and advising me was a council of many in a circle. They seemed to be seated in large wooden chairs, and some kind of ancient customs were occurring. My feelings about the prospect of living the coming lifetime were that I knew there was a lesson I wanted to learn and therefore, the prospects were positive." (Case A-325)

"Yes, I chose to be born and there seemed to be four or so entities around me advising me about the coming lifetime. My feelings about living the coming lifetime were that I wanted to. I felt that this is an important lifetime and my counselors were insistent that I must come in this time period." (Case A-302)

"Yes, I chose to be born with anticipation, as though I had been waiting for this one. No one actually helped me choose, but I felt help was available if I wanted it. I felt pleased about the prospects of living the coming lifetime, and the words 'the elements were right' flashed into my mind." (Case A-576)

"I did choose to be born, and I was with three beings to be born at a later time and we were discussing it together. I was really ready, and I seemed to know what it was all about." (Case A-476)

"Yes, I chose to be born and it was all agreed upon by a group of us. My feelings about the prospect of living the coming lifetime was that it was okay, kind of business-like. I want to accomplish something as a group (those who were advising me), and I wanted to expose myself to dissolute living and overcome it." Case A-443)

"I definitely chose to be born. The person who helped me choose was a man. We were very much in love. My feelings about the prospect of the coming lifetime was that I choose it because it was to finish a great, important part of my existence. When you asked about choosing to be born, I was looking down to earth at a fetus. The man I felt so much love for had his arm around me, and we were very excited and happy. Strange—it was similar to parents looking through a nursery window at a newborn. We were so pleased with our choice." (Case A-15)

"Yes, I chose to be born. I was waiting to return. No one actually helped me choose, but an old man was with me while I was making the choice. My feeling about the prospect of being born was that I was waiting and anxious to see if the body would be okay this time. This experience was very strange for me.

I became aware that I had been born to the same parents as my older sister Daisy, who died three months after birth because of health defects. I remembered the time in between to see if I would have another chance in this environment. That's why I was so anxious to see if the body would be okay this time." (Case A-43)

"Yes, I chose to be born, and I was helped in this choice by a council of souls. My feelings about the prospects of living the coming lifetime came through that I knew my parents needed me because they had lost a fifteen-month-old girl in a fire. So I felt eager to come to them." (Case A-48)

"Yes, I chose to be born, and I was with a group of other souls, and I somehow knew that we were regrouping. I get good feelings about the coming lifetime, because we were all planning to be together before I was born." (Case A-107)

"When you asked if I chose to be born, I did not see that there was a question. It seemed inevitable. I didn't seem aware of anyone helping me choose, but I had feelings of anticipation about the coming lifetime." (Case A-112)

"When you asked about choosing to be born, it flashed in my mind that it was something just taken for granted; 'Yes, everyone does it.' I did have schooling and consultation with teachers before my birth. I was looking forward to the experience of this coming lifetime." (Case A-140)

"Yes, I chose to be born. No one really helped me choose, but I was told I had to make the choice. I looked forward to this life because I enjoyed being able to touch things and feel things." (Case A-141)

"Yes, I chose to be born, but no one seemed to be helping me choose. I felt about this coming lifetime that it was a test, a challenge, and I was purposefully setting up a scenario for learning what I want to know." (Case A-154)

A small sub-group (about 3 percent) of the sample who chose to be born were those who apparently went against the advice of their counselors and teachers. Their reports were interesting.

"Yes, I chose to be born and it did not seem that anyone was there helping me choose. But when you asked about the prospect of living the coming lifetime, I became aware that I should have been more selective and waited a few years." (Case A-42)

"I chose to be born because I wanted to belong to a large family. I knew my brother before as a good friend. When you asked if anyone helped us choose, I became aware of someone named June that I was close to. I wanted her to come too, but she said, 'Not this time.' When you asked about the prospects of being born, someone kept saying, 'Wait till a better time. A smaller family would have more time for you.' But I felt, 'No, it has to be now.' Someone has to start first, but don't wait too long. Apparently, I was talking to the others who were telling me to wait." (Case A-191)

"Yes, I chose to be born, but I was in a hurry, and I wasn't sure of my choice. When you asked if anyone helped me choose, I became aware that someone, I'm not sure who, gave me a warning, but I felt that I had to get something done and solve something." (Case A-209)

"Yes, I did choose myself to be born. When you asked if anyone helped me choose, I became aware that someone was trying to keep me from getting born. They were warning me. My feelings about the prospect of the coming lifetime were that I had an urgent desire to get down there to *play*. But after I was born, I felt that it was so rough. The atmosphere was rude down here on earth. I had expected playing, but it was all commotion, and I longed to be back in the space where everything was light." (Case A-339)

"Yes, very clearly, I chose to be born. Some entities were trying to advise me, but I didn't listen. I was impatient to finish something I had started." (Case A-320)

"Yes, I chose to be born, but it was in panic. It was not a decision made at leisure. When you asked if anyone helped me choose, I was aware of guides that seemed to be large light beams, guiding me not to be born now—but I was determined. My feelings about the prospects of living the coming lifetime were that I wanted it and I knew my mother wasn't ready and this family wasn't right. But I had things to do and three karmic trips to complete." (Case A-493)

"When you asked if I chose to be born, I just felt drawn in and attached to the fetus. I felt that I was sent because I wanted a mother, and my only feelings were that I wanted back to my mother. This current lifetime and the period before it seemed the direct result of my childhood traumatic death in my most immediate past life." (Case A-440)

This subject had experienced death at age four in a bombing attack in Rumania in 1942. She became aware of the emotionally painful experience of roaming around the devastated area, crying for her mother.

The largest group in the sample, 67 percent, chose to be born but expressed some reluctance about living another lifetime.

"Yes, I chose to be born. I think others helped me, but no one told me to do it. It was as if I chose and I had two people I kind of was talking to about what I would do. My feelings about the prospect of living the coming lifetime were that it was okay. I was not terribly upset, nor was I anxious to be born. I knew it wouldn't be long, so I didn't mind leaving, but I kept looking back. I waited until the last minute." (Case A-7)

"Yes, I chose to be born. I talked it over with a group of friends. My feelings about the prospect of coming into the current lifetime was, 'Well, guess I'll go get stripped down some more.'" (Case A-418)

"Yes, I chose to be born, and there seemed to be a board or committee—a group of authorities to help me choose. I was not too anxious or interested in living this lifetime, but I knew I had something to do on this plane, something to accomplish. The whole feeling of birth seemed to be an annoying, unpleasant trip to accomplish something in this lifetime. I feel an urgency." (Case A-408)

"Yes, it was a difficult decision. There was a group helping me choose. They listened to what I had planned and made some suggestions. My feeling about living the coming lifetime was that I was not happy, but I knew what I was going to do was important enough to push aside my feelings of not wanting to be confined to a physical world." (Case A-431)

"When you asked if I chose to be born, I didn't want to, but I was convinced by a counselor that I needed to help with enlightenment. The man who helped me choose seemed to have a white beard and cane and was a kind of spiritual guide. When you asked about the prospect of being born, I became clearly aware that I didn't want to and was very reluctant. I even knew that I had tried to abort while in the womb." (Case A-434)

This next subject had recovered from a life-threatening illness two years before the workshop.

"I was persuaded to be born with others that I knew to tie up all residual loose ends from my most immediate life before. When you asked about helping to choose, I became aware of some old mentors of mine, three of them, but I recognized only one. When you asked about the prospects of living the coming lifetime, I had a feeling of tedium and homesickness for the place I left (not on earth), and I determined to do it right this time once and for all. I felt I wanted to go on longer with this, as it seemed I took almost too many units of learning this time around. I was given an option to leave if I got too tired, but I have already passed this up to finish. It seems I have two units to accomplish, one done and one still to go." (Case A-437)

"Yes, I chose to be born, but I kind of hemmed and hawed. It seemed there were friends helping me choose, a lot of them. They wanted me to go. I had doubts because my last life was unpleasant, and I really didn't have any pressing karma to work on. It was mighty comfortable there. I can remember talking with people on the other plane, trying to decide. I knew I had things to take care of but nothing pressing. I feel I kind of went along for the ride." (Case A-481)

"Yes, I chose to be born. There was a group talking it over, but the choice was up to me. My feelings about the prospects of living the coming lifetime was that it was like having to go to work, getting ready for the journey and packing up my energies." (Case A-482)

"Yes, I chose to be born, but very reluctantly. There were several others around me when I was deciding and they seemed to be just like me. They said they would be around to help me in the coming lifetime. When you asked about the prospect of being born, I did not want to leave the beautiful garden and my friends there." (Case A-489)

"Reluctantly, I chose to be born. There were presences around me when I was deciding, but no talking took place. My feeling about the prospect of living this lifetime was that it was not too exciting. It was more like something that had to be done to finish off a job, without the certainty that that would finish it." (Case A-490)

"Yes, I chose to be born, but somewhat reluctantly. Others were helping me choose and they seemed to be vague figures. Some were human shapes and some geometric shapes. There was a general agreement among all of us that it was somehow necessary, but I felt pushed into it." (Case A-491)

The next subject described an interesting case of choosing a body that another entity had rejected.

"Yes, I chose to be born. And someone who helped me choose was the person who first opted for the body I would have. I felt quite anxious about the prospect of living a lifetime. I seemed to have died not too long before and I was very anxious to get back into a body. I thought the time and date would give me opportunity to lead a much different life than before, where I was sort of a raunchy person." (Case A-494)

"When you asked if I chose to be born, I felt skeptical. There are images of people around me at that time, suggesting work I could do, but I felt doubtful. My feelings about living the coming lifetime were that there was a lot of work ahead and I wanted to stay where I was. I was not thrilled about living another lifetime." (Case A-524)

"Yes, I chose to be born. I felt close support, warm feelings and a lovely, comfortable feeling from a number of entities around me. It was a nice sendoff. My feelings about the prospect of living the coming lifetime were ambivalent. I felt I was above it, looking downward at prospective mother and family. I felt separation anxiety from the plane of existence I was on." (Case A-527)

"Yes, I chose to be born. There was a group of us, and they were advising me, and we were planning to go together. I felt regret about leaving where I was, and a sense of dedication for the plan to work with others." (Case A-307)

"I was offered the chance to be born and I agreed at a sort of important conference. There seemed to be an old bearded man there who was a big boss. I wanted to have a body again, so I felt happy at the prospect of living a lifetime and smiled. I wasn't happy to return as a woman. That sort of put me off, but I still elected to come." (Case A-316)

"Yes, I chose to be born. Someone helped me choose, and this person was a complete friend. He told me I would receive help. Another person also 'talked' to me. My feelings about the prospect of living the lifetime were that it was a lot of work, but I thought about the food I could eat. Before my birth there seemed to be a conference and there were feelings of deep love of one of my advisers. We talked of my learning to reach my life plan. Strong feeling of a plan." (Case A-341)

"Yes, I chose to be born. When you asked if anyone helped me choose I pictured a man in a top hat and cape. My first impression was that he was my husband (but not in appearance), and then I realized my husband would have been an infant at that time. My feelings about being born were that I was stepping into an icy stream I knew I had to cross." (Case A-350)

"When you asked if I chose to be born, I felt, 'Well, it's okay, I guess.' Someone helped me choose and he told me that these two people, my parents-to-be, would be able to give me love, stability, confidence, drive and persistence. My feeling about the prospect of being born was, 'Okay—why not?' " (Case A-351)

"When you asked if I chose to be born, I was sort of reluctant, but I know I had to go here. Others were around me when I was choosing. It was my sister and some other person, and my brother from a past life and my boyfriend in this life. When you asked about the feeling of living the coming lifetime, I didn't want to go ahead of the rest, but I had to because the 'councilmen' insisted that I show them that it would be okay. I liked the experience in the between-life state. Recognizing people was amazing!" (Case A-354)

"Yes, I chose to be born. I felt that my soulmate who was my husband in this life helped me choose. I had a feeling that I had to come back in to earth life, but I had a sense of sadness in returning to this plane." (Case A-361)

"I did choose to be born, but it was reluctantly at first. There seemed to be about five spirit counselors and they were like leaders I had known in former lifetimes. I was scared at the prospect of living this life, but I liked the woman I saw below, who would be my mother, and I wanted to make her happy. I was told by my counselors I was to be put here to find, to show, to teach, to learn. I seemed to know my friends and lovers would be like-minded people." (Case A-371)

"Yes, I chose to be born. Others helped me choose and it seemed there are friends or helpers that have a sincere interest in me. But I was ambivalent about the prospect of living this lifetime. I need to go, and once I get into it, it will be okay. But enlightenment is so nice in this plane. It is so good to see things in perspective." (Case A-398)

"Yes I chose to be born, although I felt it was going

to be a hassle. Someone helped me choose, someone more knowledgeable than I. My feelings about living the coming lifetime were that it was something that had to be done, like washing the floor when it's dirty." (Case A-285)

"Yes, I chose to be born, but it was not arranged by me, rather like a travel agent gives you a tour you can go on. When you asked if anyone helped me choose, I saw two or three friends and one was a wise-man type. My feelings about the prospect of being born were that it was like forcing yourself to jump into a pool. Entering into a fleshy state was rather an unappetizing thought." (Case A-231)

"When you asked if I chose to be born, I felt I didn't really choose, but I was prompted to by a mother figure. I clung to her in the clouds and I hesitated being born. My feelings about the prospect of living the coming lifetime were that I knew I needed to find my other half and unity. I seemed to be a little girl before I was born with long hair." (Case A-207)

"Yes, I chose to be born, and I had a number of helpers and guides helping me choose. They were very supportive. My feelings about the prospect of living the coming lifetime were that I was anxious and I expected trauma. Not so much mine, but others originally and then I would register it. I had a prior feeling of the confusion and excitability of those alive and waiting for me to be born." (Case A-204)

"When you asked if I chose to be born, it seemed as though I was in a line to be born and I got out of line. I wasn't aware of anyone helping me choose. I was having fun and joking with the others waiting to be born. I felt I would see these others again that I was with prior to birth after I was born." (Case A-198)

"I was reluctant to be born, but I did choose. Someone was telling me I really should. I didn't really want to go down and leave the cloud security and feel cold and isolated." (Case A-190)

"Yes, I reluctantly chose to be born. It seemed to be a self-decision after a review of needs. I preferred not to live the coming lifetime, but I felt it had to be." (Case A-185)

"I chose to be born because I was asked to return for additional credits by my soulmate. I seemed reluctant, but I was assured that it would be better to love more sincerely and to be appreciative." (Case A-169)

"I did choose to be born, and I wasn't aware of others helping me choose. I felt that I needed the experience of the coming lifetime, but I had misgivings about what was ahead of me." (Case A-165)

"Yes, I chose to be born, and there were several friends who were helping me choose. I was quite scared at the prospect of living the coming lifetime, but I was aware that it was a big chance." (Case A-162)

"Yes, I chose to be born, but with reluctance. There seemed to be friends around me as I chose, saying, 'Oh, come on, it will be good for you.' My feelings about the prospect of living the coming lifetime were that there was lots of work ahead, especially work on my relationship with my mother." (Case A-142)

"I chose to be born, but with reluctance. I wasn't happy about it. I saw myself as an ancient old man with a long, long beard and a robe and staff. After birth I was the same old man, only in a tiny body." (Case A-116)

"I didn't exactly choose to be born. It was just something I had to do so I could pass certain tests or learn certain lessons. It seemed like something like a computer was helping me choose, and my feelings about the prospect of living the coming lifetime were that it was a duty. I did hear people discussing an abortion or trying to talk my mother into an abortion. I felt quite determined I would be born." (Case A-104)

"Yes, I chose to be born, but I wouldn't say, however, that it was a rational or analytical decision—it was more like an intuition from an oversoul. My feelings about the prospect of being born were that I was a bit anxious and I had a familiar feeling. I know I should and I know why I should, and I know I'll be back, and I feel like this one will do its thing." (Case A-101)

"I don't really know if I chose to be born, I was aware that there were shadowy figures around me helping, but it was all very unclear." (Case A-84)

"Yes, I chose to be born, and there seemed to be some counselors around me. I felt very depressed and unhappy. Tears ran down my cheeks here during the hypnosis when you asked about the feelings about the prospect of living the coming lifetime." (Case A-55)

"Yes, I chose to be born, and there were others around teaching and guiding me. But I felt very depressed at the prospect of living another lifetime. I didn't want to, but I knew I needed the experience." (Case A-51)

"Yes, I chose to be born. It seemed my present husband and I decided. But my feelings about the prospect of being in this lifetime were of anger. I felt shocked and stifled at the prospect of being in a body once more." (Case A-46)

"Yes, I reluctantly chose to be born. I felt I was put in a white chamber like an exit chute, or a high-diving board. I seemed to have guides around me, but that was all I was aware of. I felt anxiety and fear of failure when I thought about the coming lifetime,

but I was promised that I was to receive help."
(Case A-22)

"Yes, I chose to be born. No one seemed to tell me
to be born, although someone was there seeming to say
that they are available to help, but I didn't ask for
help. I felt ambivalent about the prospect of living the
coming lifetime." (Case A-21)

"Yes, I reluctantly chose to be born. Someone
helped me choose, and he seemed to be a mentor or
guide, but he didn't come to earth on this trip with
me. I felt very reluctant about the prospect of living
the coming lifetime, and I hung back to the very last
moment before entering the fetus." (Case A-14)

Nineteen percent of all my subjects resisted the
birth experience to the point where they said they
either did not choose to be born or were not aware
of making a choice. In many ways these cases are
close to those of the subjects who chose reluctantly.

"No, I didn't choose to be born. There was someone
insisting that it was time to return. I felt very reluctant to live another lifetime because it was very pleasant on the cloud. But a voice was insisting that I
needed additional experience." (Case A-277)

"No, it seemed as though I didn't choose to be born,
but was forced by others to be born. It seemed there
was someone higher up or others insisting. I just
didn't want to be born at all." (Case A-180)

"No, I didn't choose to be born, and it seemed that
I had no choice. I wasn't aware of anyone helping me
choose. My feelings about the prospect of living this
lifetime were that I had goofed this time because I
should have been male." (Case A-201)

"No, I didn't choose to be born, because I didn't
want to do it. I felt as though someone or some persons
were forcing me into it. My feelings about the pros-

pects of living another lifetime were that I was really pissed off." (Case A-208)

"No, I didn't choose to be born. I had the feeling that something or someone controlled my birth, but I couldn't understand any more about it. I didn't want to go through another lifetime again, but I felt like I needed to learn to love. I felt like it was a recurring lesson and I had to come back again, and again and again." (Case A-394)

"I was very resistant to the idea of choosing to be born, but I know I had to make the decision myself. My feelings about the prospect of living another lifetime were that it was really a drag. This surprises me because I love living so much." (Case A-301)

"No, I didn't choose to be born. It seems as though I tried to make more decisions and be ready to teach or guide, but I needed help myself. When you asked if anyone helped me choose, I became aware that there were two helpers who were quite determined that I come back, and try to make more decisions and be ready to teach or guide in a time of stress to come. My feelings about the prospect of living a lifetime were that I didn't want to fulfill the duties of earth life. I liked being taught on another plane, and I wanted to avoid contact with other earthlings." (Case A-557)

"No, I didn't choose to be born, and I wasn't aware of anyone helping. All I knew was that I liked where I was. Tears were falling on my cheeks, here in the hypnosis session, and I don't know why. Many visions flashed in and out of my mind's eye, but again I don't know why. I only knew that I didn't want to be on earth again." (Case A-509)

"I didn't get any answer to the question if I chose to be born, or if anyone helped me choose. My feelings about the prospect of being born was that I wanted to get out of wherever I was, because I didn't understand the place. I really wanted so much to know why I chose to be born, but I couldn't get anywhere. I was in a place of all whiteness. Sort of pure white heads with blank, bland faces. I think I wanted to be back on earth again, because I was afraid of where I was. I was more familiar with earth." (Case A-499)

"When you asked if I chose to be born, I felt that I didn't, because I just wanted to zip around the universe as a beam of light. I did not want to come, but it seems I was ordered to. My only feeling about the prospect of living another lifetime was, 'Here we go again!'" (Case A-487)

"When you asked if I chose to be born, I felt that I had to. I didn't really want to. The others, the wiser ones made me do it. I didn't feel enthusiastic about living another lifetime. When I was free in space, I was confined in a golden triangle, and it seemed the only way out was to be born again." (Case A-464)

"No, I didn't choose to be born, and I wasn't aware of others around me. I only knew I didn't want to live another lifetime because I only died a short time ago and I needed rest." (Case A-453)

"No, I didn't choose to be born. I felt I had just died in a war, and was looking for some place. Then I felt pulled to my parents. I didn't have anyone helping me choose. My feelings about the prospect of living another lifetime were apprehensive. I did not want to be born." (Case A-148)

"No, I didn't choose to be born, but something just told me I had to. I didn't want to live this coming lifetime, but I knew I had to come back." (Case A-129)

"No, I didn't choose to be born, but others were telling me I should. I didn't want to live this coming

lifetime, and I said to someone, 'They are so poor.' "
(Case A-134)

"I don't know if I chose to be born or not, and I
wasn't aware of anyone helping me choose. I had no
apparent feeling about the prospect of living the coming lifetime, but when I was born I had the feeling
of, 'Well, I'm back again,' expressed in a rather resigned attitude." (Case A-121)

"I didn't choose to be born. I had a feeling of
being pointed at when you asked if anyone helped me
choose. I seemed to be unaware of what was happening. All my imagery is in vivid color and flowing
lines similar to curling cigarette smoke. I have no
distinct visual perceptions. Essentially the feelings I
had on this trip were of not knowing what was
happening." (Case A-111)

"No, I don't think I chose to be born. I got emotional when you asked that. When you asked if anyone
helped me choose, I felt blank. When you asked about
the prospect of living another lifetime, my feelings
were mixed. First I dreaded it and then I thought
I'd like it." (Case A-99)

"No, I didn't choose to be born and I wasn't aware
of anyone helping me. I was not enthused at the
prospect of living another lifetime, but a higher
authority decreed it." (Case A-69)

"No, I didn't choose to be born and I wasn't aware
of others helping me. All I felt was a strong feeling of
fear." (Case A-66)

"No, I didn't choose to be born, but there were
others around me. They seemed to be unknown voices
or energy sources giving reasons for entering the
body. My attitude toward the prospect of living another lifetime was, 'Well, if I must.' " (Case A-37)

"No, I didn't choose to be born. When you asked if
anyone helped me choose I think someone did, but

I don't know who. I didn't want to be born. When you asked about the prospect of living another lifetime, I felt very bad emotionally. It was frightening. I didn't really have any images of spirits choosing where I was to go. Just feelings. I was happy on my cloud and didn't want to leave it." (Case A-18)

An additional group of subjects (5 percent) did not answer the questions, but described their experiences under the hypnosis. They often described experiencing colors or dream-like images instead of responses to my questions.

"In the beginning of the trip I knew what you were going to ask before you asked. I saw the three pictures before you even began to speak. The first picture was just a facial portrait, but I knew what I was wearing. The majority of the rest of the trip was very sensory-oriented. I felt as though I was on a rollercoaster. Then I felt my hands were numb, they were tingling. On awakening, my hands were red and the veins distended." (Case A-119)

"When you mentioned bright light I saw it and felt it. Then a large male hand pushed into my vision and blackness intrudes. I didn't get any answers to the rest of your questions after the black hand." (Case A-115)

"When you took us to the age of five years, I felt a frightening experience right here in this room when you were hypnotizing us. At one point I was having a nightmare and after awakening it continued. There was a large, fuzzy black man-shape moving into the room. I awoke and he continued to come until I screamed another time. I heard a beautiful voice calling my name several times. I was convinced I was awake!" (Case A-113. This subject did not scream or even move during this experience.)

"Before birth I was in a different dimension. It was

very clear, very deep, and very colorful. I was not alive—I was free and without pain or anything physical. Choosing to live again was like children taking turns going down a long slide. You climbed into a white puff. It was somewhat potluck where I would come out. Some of it depended on the timing when one would climb into the white puff. I didn't know anyone in particular, I just knew everyone in general." (Case A-106)

"I'm sorry but I got no answers to your questions. The feeling I had was of being all alone. I saw no one. During the birth-canal experience I felt frightened and alone, and cold. The smell of ozone came to me from the time we started the trip." (Case A-105)

It's interesting to me to note that the smell of ozone was reported by about 10 percent of my subjects, beginning with the initial instructions on the birth trip. All these subjects were hypnotized in different groups, so it could not have been suggestion that created the smell of ozone. Could it have been the delivery-room smell?

"I was resistant to recalling this. I was very deep but once an image came in I became resistant, although I heard your voice." (Case A-89)

"I came out of trance as soon as you mentioned being born into this life. I felt a brief moment of being confined in the birth canal, which was a fleshy tunnel. Then I was wide awake." (Case A-88)

"I blanked out on all this and I woke up. I wanted to leave the room as you asked of my mother and father and karmic acquaintances. I couldn't get very much and what I got was this feeling of heavy resentment, so I just withdrew." (Case A-86)

"I wasn't sure if I wanted to be born, and when you asked if anyone helped me choose, I saw an image of a moth who spoke me into physical form, using different sounds. I saw unusually vivid colors, an intense purple-red." (Case A-516)

To summarize, 81 percent of my subjects said that they themselves chose to be born. Nineteen percent of the subjects reported that either they were unaware of the choice or they got no clear answer to the question. Both of these groups agreed that others helped them in the process of choosing another lifetime. Of those reporting counselors in the time before birth, 59 percent of my subjects mentioned more than one counselor. It was interesting to me that 10 percent of the subjects reported people in their current lifetime counseling them before birth. Some would have a mother or father counseling, some would have relatives who had died prior to their birth, some would have people they would know later in the coming lifetime. Oddly, there seemed to be no distinction between people who were alive at the time the birth was being decided upon and people who were dead or not yet born. In the world between lifetimes, our chronological time system and whether one is physically alive or dead seem of relatively little importance.

Forty-one percent of my subjects reported that they couldn't identify who their advisers or counselors were, or weren't aware of having any. They were just aware of instructions and counseling. Many of these subjects reported that they were told they would receive guidance and advice once they were alive in the body chosen for them.

Interestingly, only 0.1 percent of my subjects reported God or some other deity form as the force that led them into birth. This is unusual in a culture where we clearly have an image of a hierarchical God-like figure who controls our destiny after death, and presumably before birth. Instead, most of the advisers my subjects reported were friends and others in their peer group. Even those who described spirit guides indicated that these spirit guides were not necessarily superior figures, but rather colleagues who were not alive in a body before my subjects were born.

Sixty-eight percent of my subjects felt reluctant, anxious, or resigned to the prospect of living another lifetime. Eight percent had no response to the question of their feelings at the prospect of living another lifetime. Only 26 percent of my subjects looked forward to the coming lifetime, many of these subjects reporting that they had planned carefully, and felt they would have help from the other dimension in achieving their goals in this life. It was hope of achievement and not pleasure that made life worth living for them.

So death was experienced as pleasant by 90 percent of these subjects, but being born—living another lifetime—was unhappy and frightening. What a strange reversal of what I had expected! Do we love and value life so much as we publicly profess to in this culture?

Perhaps life was more pleasant in the past. Maybe I was tapping the cultural confusion brought by events in the last half of the twentieth century.

IV

CHOOSING THE TWENTIETH CENTURY AND CHOOSING ONE'S SEX

When I asked my subjects if they chose the twentieth century to experience a lifetime for a reason, I had no idea what responses I would get. I was just curious about whether this time period would be regarded as a fruitful time to experience physical life, or if it would be seen negatively by my subjects. The fact that so many of my subjects wished to stay in the between-life state, and reluctantly agreed to be born, suggested that I would get many negative responses to the question of choosing the twentieth century. Perhaps my subjects were reluctant because this was a difficult time period, and if I had asked about birth into other time periods they might have had more positive responses.

My subjects' response to this question surprised me. Many of the subjects, 41 percent, got no impression in response to this question, or simply reported "No." Perhaps the very concept of a time period refers to earthly consciousness. Space and time are different for us when we are dreaming than when we are awake. In a dream, we may be in our childhood home one moment, and at the office next week in the next moment. Right brain time is experienced differently; when we are daydreaming or working creatively, time rushes by us. When people are stoned on marijuana, time slows as thoughts drift through the right brain. How much time does it take to dream? It's hard for us to guess.

The left brain—our word-brain temporal lobe that is functioning when we are focused in the physical, "real" world—is left behind by my subjects when they are lying on the floor listening to my voice. Memory is indifferent to "real world time," and our fifth birthday is remembered more vividly than last Tuesday at the office.

So perhaps the very phrase "time period" is not meaningful to the right brain of my hypnotized subjects. If the part of us that "reincarnates" is our memory of sensory experiences, loves and hates, longings and memory of our accomplishments, then perhaps it can be said that the right brain lobes are our true memory bank that flows with us through many lifetimes. After we die, we may well forget such workaday details as our names, addresses, who was President, the name of our country or our race. The language skills we are so proud of in our earthly life may be the least important to our soul or entity self.

If we are here on earth to learn, as my subjects so strongly suggest, then it is the learning of the heart, the emotions, that is important. "Suffer the little children to come unto me, for of them is the kingdom of God." The wisdom of Jesus suggests that when children learn language, reason and the rules of the tribe they happen to be born into, perhaps they are shutting away the wisdom of the feeling self, the right brain knowing.

So "time" may mean little when we are not focused in a physical body, when we are "dead." Yet I wanted to know if the apocalypse predicted in the historical Christian religion would be reflected in my subjects' responses. Are we all to disappear in cataclysms at the end of the twentieth century?

First let's look at the answers from subjects who didn't choose a time period to be born.

Many of those who reported that they had no choice of the twentieth century, or did not choose it specifically, also had difficulty in choosing to be born.

"When you asked if I chose to be born, choice did not seem to be involved. The question whether anyone helped seemed irrelevant to me. I was indifferent about the prospect of being born. When you asked about the time period of the twentieth century, again choice did not seem to be a factor." (Case B-23)

"No, I didn't choose to be born, and I don't know who it was who helped me choose, but some people were there. I felt okay about the prospect of being born. When you asked about the twentieth century, all that flashed in my mind was that it was just supposed to be then." (Case B-26)

"No, I didn't choose to be born, and I didn't want to be born, but others were there saying I should. I felt forced when you asked about this time period, and the word came into my mind, 'No.'" (Case B-54)

"I don't think I chose to be born, and I feel I must have been told I had to be born. My feelings about birth were a feeling of crushing sensations in my chest. When you asked about choosing the twentieth century, I felt I had no choice." (Case B-113)

"No, I didn't choose to be born, but someone was

clearly deciding for me. I did not want to leave where I was to be born. When you asked about the twentieth century, I felt it was already decided." (Case A-34)

"You asked if I chose to be born, and it flashed in my mind, 'No.' There was a group telling me I should be born, but I didn't like it. I had the feeling that I had to. I'm not sure whether I chose this time period or not." (Case B-76)

Some other subjects chose to be born, but still got no impression of why the twentieth century was the period they would be alive.

"Yes, I chose to be born, but somewhat reluctantly. It seems there was a group of people advising me, but one person seemed to insist that I go. I was somewhat apprehensive. I don't recall any answer for the question about choosing the twentieth century." (Case A-12)

"Yes, I chose to be born and no one helped me and I felt good about the prospect of being born. It flashed in my mind, the words 'No,' or 'indefinite,' when you asked about the twentieth century." (Case A-6)

"I chose to be born, and I wasn't aware of anyone helping me choose. I was anxious and wanted to be here. But when you asked about the twentieth century, it flashed in my mind that it was just time to return, nothing else." (Case A-381)

"I didn't exactly choose to be born, I had to be coaxed and encouraged. There were some shadowy, hooded figures of older people advising me. I had a feeling of dread about the prospects of the coming lifetime and the feeling was, 'Oh, do I have to go through all of that again?' When you asked if I chose the twentieth century, the answer flashed, 'No, it was just time to go, because rest time was over.'" (Case B-81)

Of those subjects answering yes to the question of

whether or not they chose the twentieth century to live the coming lifetime, I was surprised to find that a majority (51 percent) chose this time period because of its great potential for spiritual growth. Perhaps there are some evidences of earth changes to come in these responses, but the positive aspects of this time period are stressed. Thirty-four percent of the subjects expressed this in very similar words.

"Yes, I chose the twentieth century because it is the time of earth changes, and the raising of levels of consciousness." (Case B-5)

"Expansion of consciousness will be great in last half of twentieth century and I can learn a lot." (Case A-76)

"I chose the twentieth century because this century is the dawning of a new age of awareness, and many, many souls are going to transcend to another plane of oneness." (Case A-379)

"I chose the last half of the twentieth century because it seems conducive to the job I must do for myself, because of the oneness of all spirits in the new age." (Case A-377)

"I chose the last half of the twentieth century to help the awareness of togetherness moving forward in this time period." (Case A-383)

"I chose the last half of the twentieth century to be alive because more advanced spirits are being born and we are closer to obtaining world peace and a sense of the total self of mankind." (Case A-384)

"This is an important and exciting age to be born into." (Case A-415)

"Yes, the last half of the twentieth century is the time of enlightenment I have been waiting for to live another lifetime." (Case B-91)

"I chose the last half of the twentieth century because it is the beginning of a new age, and there is more acceptance of growing consciousness." (Case A-4)

"I chose this time period because it is one of great awakening." (Case A-17)

"I chose this time period because there are many souls coming together now, and my higher self was aware of this." (Case A-415)

"I chose this time period because it is the new birth of a golden age." (Case A-47)

"This is an important time for life on this plane—consciousness will be raised to a higher plane." (Case B-68)

"This is the most important time of change, and I want to be here for it." (Case B-69)

"This is a time of great change and I want to be here now." (Case B-71)

"I chose the last half of the twentieth century because the evolution of mankind's will will move very fast in this time period." (Case B-72)

"I chose the last half of the twentieth century because of the transition of history from a religious to a scientific view, and at the end of this age, a spiritual awakening." (Case B-88)

"It seemed that this is a period of major transition to a higher level of consciousness." (Case B-89)

"I felt this time period was an intense historical point, as opposed to the past, a climactic time." (Case B-90)

"Yes, I chose this time because very monumental changes are occurring and will occur." (Case A-476)

"Because it's a period of great change." (Case A-21)

"There is an increasing awareness of the spiritual element in Western cultures, and I felt I could aid this in the last half of the twentieth century." (Case A-114)

"This time period is one that is open to spiritual growth." (Case B-36)

"There is a feeling of brightness associated with the end of the twentieth century. This came to me strongly under hypnosis." (Case B-8)

While the majority of my subjects stressed the "new age" theme, another 30 percent of the subjects responding to the question about choosing the last half of the twentieth century, apparently did so primarily for personal reasons. Generally, this was because other important people whom they had known in former lives would be alive at this time.

"It's the only time my fiancé and I could be together in our sex roles that we had chosen." (Case B-7)

"I felt my reason for this particular life in this time period was to have contact with particular people who also chose this time period." (Case B-12)

"I chose this time period to fulfill the life of my older sister. Her body was inferior, and she died three months after her birth because of health defects. I seem to be her. I remember the time in between before I was born to my mother as her second daughter, and I seem to be waiting in this between-life period to see if I would have another chance in this environment." (Case A-43)

"I chose this time period because all conditions seemed correct." (Case B-87)

"I chose the last half of the twentieth century to be with my husband." (Case B-86)

"I came in this time period because certain other people I needed to work out relationships with would also be alive at this time." (Case B-70)

"I came this time to get to know my mother better who was my best friend in a previous life and she was alive in this time period." (Case B-55)

"It would afford me the people and opportunities I needed." (Case B-33)

"I came in this time period to find someone, though I don't know exactly who it is I am to find. I haven't met this person yet." (Case A-32)

"I chose this last half of the twentieth century to be near someone I knew from before." (Case A-249)

"I chose this time period because of a strong feeling of wanting to be with children I had had in past lives. But they are not my children now. They are in other relationships to me." (Case B-111)

"I came into this time period to be near my mother." (Case B-99)

"I came in this time period to correct past errors and to work out my guilt about certain relationships." (Case A-57)

"The twentieth century was a better time to develop my knowledge and to share with the world." (Case A-33. This subject is a research chemist.)

Other subjects had a more personal approach. Several subjects felt that they had something special to teach, and so chose this time period to be alive.

"I chose the twentieth century because they were ready to hear what I had to bring to them, at least around 1980 on." (Case A-386)

"The years 1950 to 2000 in America would offer the greatest possibilities and opportunities in this life. I had something to teach." (Case A-478)

My estimate that my subjects would describe the last half of the twentieth century as a period of difficult living was not borne out by the data. Only 4 percent of those answering the question described this time period as an unusually difficult one, and these subjects seemed to emphasize the positive aspect of being able to learn a good deal, as well as describing difficulties.

One subject, an older woman, felt that she chose the twentieth century because it was the last of the kind of era where she could devote herself to nurturing a family in the traditional female role. She reported, "I sensed troubled times and it was the last of a kind of era. It was rough times, but I felt I had more opportunity to make people happy in this time."

"I felt I chose this time period because there was a great world turmoil toward the end of this century." (Case B-56)

"I chose the last half of the twentieth century because it was a stressful time, but essential education would be available to me." (Case A-41)

"This time is a time of trial." (Case A-60)

"I chose the last half of the twentieth century to live in a time of trials and tribulations, a period of time I knew would be educating." (Case A-63)

"I chose this time period because of much political and social strife." (Case A-65)

Another small group, 4 percent of the subjects, reported that they chose this time period, as well as their sex as a female, because of special opportunities available in this time with a change in status of women. These subjects seem to have needed to work out the female half of their entities, but had delayed this until a time when to be a woman was less socially inhibiting than it had been in earlier time periods.

"I came as a woman into the twentieth century to find the potential of the female for spiritual and sexual growth. This time frame allows more freedom for a woman to experience life totally." (Case A-385)

"I must have needed to work out the female part of my entity. I chose this era because women will make great advances in my lifetime and I will help in that advance." (Case A-186)

"I chose the last half of the twentieth century because it was a time to have women lead in this period." (Case A-48)

"Yes, I chose this time period because women have more freedom now to do their own thing." (Case B-83)

"I chose the twentieth century to be a woman because women are going beyond domination now." (Case A-103)

"I had to realize my own inner strengths and independence, and this time period was relevant due to women's liberation. A time for women to find strengths, influence and independence in a man's world." (Case A-454)

Another 14 percent of those responding to the question gave individual responses that could not be categorized as a new age, period of hard times, time to learn or to teach, or a time to experience life as a woman. A few of these reported that they chose this time period because of the exploration of life beyond earth.

"I chose this time period because it was the era of outer space. (I don't know why this came into my mind under hypnosis, but that's what came to me.)" (Case B-19)

"I chose this time period because it is the age of man's physical leaving of his planet." (Case A-80)

The other responses were unique to each person, though there were only fourteen such unique responses.

"Communication was the only word or image that came into my mind when you asked about the reason for being born in this century." (Case B-37)

"I chose this lifetime because of something political, but I don't really understand what." (Case B-41)

"I chose this time period because of the electro-magnetic conditions." (Case B-63)

"There seemed to be no great turmoil in this period." (Case A-2)

"I came in this time period because I would have a lot of prosperity." (Case A-23)

"I chose this time period because it is the completion of a cycle. I think it's a cycle for all of us, though I'm not clear on this." (Case A-54)

In summary, it seems clear that the majority of my subjects who did get an answer to the question, "Did you choose the last half of the twentieth century to experience life for a reason?" answered in very similar ways. Over 70 percent of all the subjects mentioned that the last half of the twentieth century would be characterized by a new development of spiritual awareness. It is interesting to me that many of these subjects described a growing awareness of oneness, a coming together of individuals to transcend their individuality and to become aware that they are linked on higher planes. While there was some feeling that the last half of the twentieth century would be characterized by earth changes and some social upheavals, the positive aspects of this time period were emphasized. In general, my subjects felt that this era is one that will allow great developments because of the tremendous opportunities to learn in a time when science has supplanted more primitive religions, and when there is a growing awareness of the spiritual nature of man.

The most enthusiastic sub-group of those who chose this time period were the subjects who felt eager to come in this time period, had planned their life carefully, and felt that they were here to assist in a new development in mankind's history. They felt that what they had learned in other planes was now something they could teach on the earth plane as well. However, a substantial minority of the subjects (30 percent) apparently were still concerned with working out their individual karmic relationships and chose this time period because others that they had known in past lives were also planning to be alive now. Often these subjects were ones who were most reluctant to be born, and expressed little enthusiasm for the tasks that lay ahead.

Choosing One's Sex for the Coming Lifetime

I included the question, "Did you choose your sex before you were born?" because sexuality is such an explosive issue in our time. We seem to be divided into hostile camps as the movement to free women from their restrictive social role changes deep habits and beliefs in our culture.

I knew that my subjects often experienced past lives as the opposite sex. Over 2,000 hypnotic subjects had reported this phenomenon. In the right brain the "self" is neither male nor female, and "remembers" the experience of childbirth and the experience of leading men in battle. Is our sexuality, which we consider a deeply innate part of our personality, more of a left-brain superficial aspect of our being? If it is, are there still important lessons to be learned in a physical body that can best be learned by being male, or being female?

Of those subjects responding to this question, 24 percent said that they felt they had not chosen their sex, or that the sex in the coming lifetime was not of importance.

"No, I didn't choose my sex, it was just time to return, so I took what was available." (Case A-381)

"I don't think it mattered which sex I had." (Case B-28)

"My sex was not important for my purpose." (Case B-80)

"I didn't choose my sex, and if I had I would have chosen to be a boy to please the family. I just needed to be with these people." (Case B-71)

Twenty-eight percent of my subjects were males, and responded in various ways to the question of why they chose a male lifetime for their current life. It is hard to categorize these responses, but the one that occurred most frequently is that the male is dominant in our society and, therefore, they chose to be male because it would meet their purposes better.

"I chose to be a male to physically build objects, houses, etc." (Case A-23)

"Yes, I chose to be a male to lessen the shock of physical sensation." (Case B-63)

"I chose to be a male to develop a sense of mastery inside my character." (Case B-56)

"Well, I didn't really choose my sex, but I was pleased to find I would be a male this time. I had been the opposite sex in the most immediate past life, and I led a miserable life." (Case A-57)

"I wanted to be a female for pleasure, but I chose the male sex for this lifetime because for me the tests would be harder." (Case B-25)

"Yes, I chose to be a male because of my wife. I came to this life to help my wife solve a problem, and she had chosen to be female." (Case A-27)

"I chose to be a male, because it was easier as a male to participate in scientific endeavor, and I wanted in this lifetime to be a part of the twentieth-century science revolution." (Case A-19)

"Yes, I was male in my last life and I wanted to continue where I left off. I wanted to become a scientist because in my last life I had that same wish, but I died young as a soldier." (Case A-35)

"I chose to be a male because I was going into a

male-dominated society, so I could better do my work as a male." (Case A-21)

"It seemed that I chose to be a male because otherwise I probably would have gotten custody of my children after the divorce and would not have evolved into a real relationship with them." (Case A-379)

"I chose to be a male because I felt I had sexual problems as a male to work out." (Case A-2)

Forty-eight percent of my subjects chose to be female in their current lifetimes. Nearly a third of these reported the primary reason for choosing a female role was to have children. But many other reasons also surfaced for this choice of sex.

"I chose to be a woman, because I felt being female would make it easier to help people. They would accept help easier from a woman than from a man." (Case A-7)

"I chose to be a woman because female is more loving, expressive, in touch with self. I feel the female part of myself is better able to reflect this." (Case A-384)

"I did choose my sex. At first, I wanted to be a male, but I changed to a female because I could be gentler." (Case A-17)

"I chose to be a female because it is a better channel for creative love." (Case A-45)

"I chose to be a woman because it is time for me to give birth to tomorrow's explorers of life." (Case A-47)

"I chose to be a woman because a man cannot give as fully as a woman." (Case A-11)

"I chose to be a woman because my mate wanted us to be the same sex we were in 1503." (Case A-15)

"I chose to be a female because my parents would accept that more easily than if I were a male." (Case A-387)

"When you asked if I chose my sex, I had the distinct impression that this was maybe the first life I've led as a woman, so it seemed novel. It was as if my friends thought it would be a great joke on me to send me out as a woman this time. This was a strange impression." (Case A-439)

"I chose to be a woman because my parents needed another girl, and because it was a time to have women lead." (Case A-48)

"I came as a woman in the twentieth century to find the potential of the female for spiritual and sexual growth. This time frame allows more freedom for a woman to experience life today." (Case A-385)

"I chose to be a woman because it is easier to make people happy by being a female." (Case B-27)

"I chose to be a woman in this lifetime to fulfill the needs of a loving wife and mother at a time when it is becoming obsolete." (Case A-63)

"I chose to be a woman only because my fiancé had chosen his life and I had to be of the appropriate sex so that we could be together." (Case B-7)

"I chose to be a woman in this lifetime because I was male in the previous life." (Case B-55)

"I didn't really choose my sex, but I felt being female was the only opportunity to be where I wanted to be." (Case A-1)

"I chose to be a woman for this lifetime because women will be stronger in this period." (Case B-11)

"I chose to be a woman in this life to have children and to be reunited with past souls. There are several of them that I wish to give birth to." (Case A-22)

"I chose my sex simply to be with my husband. He and I were deciding before we were born what our roles would be." (Case A-47)

"I definitely chose to be a woman because I wanted to be spoiled and fragile this time." (Case B-95)

The answers seemed to show that apparently it is easier to lead, to demonstrate mastery, as a male. But it is easier to learn and to show love when one is in a female body and female social role.

Yet the striking result from the answers to this question in my survey is that not one of my 750 subjects felt their "true, inner self" to be either male or female. The growing entity self, moving and gathering experiences through many lifetimes, is truly above sexual distinctions and must incorporate both experiences—yin and yang, male and female—to reach deeper understanding.

V

WHY ARE WE HERE ON EARTH? HAVE WE KNOWN OUR FAMILY AND FRIENDS IN OTHER LIFETIMES?

Why are we living? This question is so profoundly important that I hesitated to include it in my birth trip. Most of us, including me, would like to know the answer, but it slips away from us. Our purposes change as we move through the currents, eddies and still backwaters of the river of life. At times, our purposes are the same as others around us. In another phase of our life, our purposes seem like a cross-current running against the purposes of those closest to us.

The religions of the world offer answers to this question, but these, too, change with different eras of history. Most of the world religions began with the mystical insights of a great leader. But as these insights are translated into priesthoods and hierarchies, they seem to thin out into a more mundane wisdom. For much of mankind, through much of human history, the purpose of life is to conform to the rules of the tribe, worship an unknowable God, and avoid conflict with the social order at any given time or place. "Keep your nose clean and don't rock the boat" are probably the oldest bits of moral wisdom in human history.

A majority of my subjects under hypnosis reported their impression that the last half of the twentieth century will mark a new stage in the spiritual development of mankind. What will be this new spiritual development? We have known of the Golden Rule for two thousand years—Do unto others as you would have them do unto you—but as I observed the world, we had yet to put this into practice. The practical side of my nature told me that our purpose seems to be to maximize our individual portions of material goods, power and self-esteem. Yet my cynical side also noticed that the more we had of material goods and power, and the esteem of our fellow tribesman, the more we searched for that something more.

So I included the question, "What is your purpose in choosing this coming lifetime?" in my survey.

Those subjects of mine who were unable to remember what they had experienced because they went too deep, or who did not get any answers to this question, felt particularly frustrated because they were looking for their purpose. A few subjects were able to get answers to the rest of the questions on the birth experience, but still blanked out on their purpose.

"When you asked the purpose for living this coming lifetime, I became aware that there was something in store for me, but my purpose is as yet unknown." (Case A-65)

"I had the feeling that before birth it was discussed with me what the purpose was. But when I was launched, so to speak, with my two unknown companions helping me, I was not allowed to know anything about having friends from past lives or the purpose of this life." (Case A-364)

"I knew there was a reason why I was here, but couldn't really remember why." (Case A-373)

Of those responding to this question, 25 percent of my subjects said that the purpose of living their current lifetime was to gain additional experience. Some examples of this type of response follow:

"In the past life I experienced under hypnosis, I lived in a mass society as an Asian, and I was a contemplative monk. No one saw or heard me. This lifetime now is to develop ego." (Case B-90)

"My purpose is simply to advance and achieve as best I can, just to live and experience." (Case A-382)

"Why I was born is beyond me. I certainly didn't want to. Maybe I'm here to learn how to like it." (Case A-429. This subject definitely did not want to return, but was reluctantly persuaded to do so by a group of other people.)

"When you asked about the purpose, all that came was something about experiencing physical reality once more in order to learn." (Case A-287)

"My purpose in this lifetime is simply to learn more about myself." (Case B-28)

"My purpose came to experience life as a non-important person, but to be part of the twentieth-century science revolution." (Case A-19)

"My purpose was to fulfill the needs of a loving wife and mother, and to live in a time of trials when I would learn much." (Case A-63)

"When you asked the purpose of this lifetime, I got a feeling of lots of confusion. I think I am here to learn the reason for the confusion." (Case A-1)

"Before my birth there was a conference and I had a feeling of deep love from one of my advisors. He talked of my learning to reach my life plan. When you asked about purpose, all I felt was a strong feeling of a plan, and this was just part of it." (Case A-341)

"When you asked the purpose of this life, I heard a voice insisting that I needed additional experience." (Case A-277)

"I seem to have died not too long before and I was very anxious to get back into a body. I thought this time and date would give me the opportunity to lead a much different life than before, when I was a sort of raunchy person. So I chose a crowded existence with many experiences." (Case A-494)

"When you asked the purpose, I got the impression that there were almost too many units of learning this time around. I became aware that I was given an option to leave if I got too tired, but I had already passed this up to finish the last two units, one I am doing and one still to go. I don't know quite what these are, but that's the impression that came through clearly." (Case A-437)

"I was anxious to come back into a body and get started, as my purpose was that there would be much to learn and many experiences, good and bad, to go through." (Case A-197)

"Before I was born, I saw myself as something, and several other somethings like me indicated that I should be born and be able to learn to make choices, and to use this ability to overcome the barrier between three-dimensional reality and basic reality, a blending. I am to try and experience this in this lifetime." (Case A-189)

"When you asked about the purpose of my life, I felt it was a mission to gather the strands in a com-

plex life and successfully be Icarus riding the chariot
to the sun without fear, holding up many reins."
(Case A-156)

"When you asked the purpose, it flashed in my mind
that I thought I was a little too special, and I'm here
this time to work through that mighty ego." (Case
A-268)

Eighteen percent of the sample said that their purpose in this lifetime was to be with one or several
other people they had known in past lives in order
to work out their relationships.

"When I was choosing to be born, I was aware that
one of my children was with me in this time between
lives. I felt strongly that my purpose in this life was
to produce a great leader, and this one of my sons
will be a great leader, and produce social changes.
I don't want my other children to know about this,
and I wasn't aware of it until the hypnosis, that my
strongest purpose was just to give birth to this son."
(Case A-187)

"When you asked a purpose, I understood why I
did choose my parents. It was to help them in the
working of their karmas. I felt like I was to be used
as the instrument to help my parents." (Case A-151)

"I realize now that part of my purpose this time
is to be aware of my mother's feelings toward me and
learn to love her anyway. Oh boy, is that a toughie!"
(Case A-242)

"When you asked the purpose of this life it was
unclear to me except that I can accomplish it. I also
flashed on the fact that I am looking for certain people that I have known in past lives. One is someone
I was close to in the Mayan culture. Another will be a
child of mine. I'm waiting for this child, and I'm very
excited about it. And I don't know if it will be a boy
or a girl, but now I know it's someone I've known in a

past life. I am also glad to have been with another lover who on the second past life-hypnosis trip was with me briefly, but had only met me when I died that time. I realize that he is now very dear to me. But it surprised me because under the hypnosis I became aware he doesn't seem to be the main reason this time around. It's just always nice to be with him again. I think the man from the Mayan lifetime and the child are the ones I'm waiting for." (Case A-391)

"When you asked the purpose, I felt strongly this life was chosen to experience rejection by my mother and sister, and my final detachment so that I can get on with my spiritual tasks." (Case A-338)

"I knew that my purpose was to meet again the man who helped me choose to be born, and this was to finish a great, important part of my existence with him." (Case A-15)

"When you asked the purpose, I realized it was to establish a new relationship with people I owed from damage I did to them in past lives. I am certainly aware now that my husband in this life is an alcoholic, and I understand that I must help him because I was unkind to him in a past life." (Case B-11)

"When you asked the purpose of this lifetime, I felt strongly that I came this time to be a nurturer. I thought the world needed a mother and I chose a role of raising a specific family of satisfied kids— people I'd known in past lives." (Case B-64)

"When you asked the purpose, it came clearly into my mind that it was to make up to some people for the hurt I had caused them in former lives." (Case B-70)

"When you asked the purpose, I became aware that it was to find someone, and that I chose to be a male so that I might find this person. No other information about this came through." (Case A-32)

"When asked the purpose for this lifetime, it came through clearly to me that someone needed help, and that the rest were already here. (Rest who? I really don't understand why this came into my mind, but I'm writing it down anyway.)" (Case B-75)

"When you asked the purpose of this lifetime, it came through very clearly, it was to take care of my mother." (Case B-99)

"Apparently my purpose in this lifetime is a strong feeling of wanting to be with my children whom I've known in past lives." (Case B-111)

"I felt the reason for this particular life in this time period was to have contacts with other people who also chose this time period. Somehow it was group effort." (Case A-527)

Another 18 percent of my subjects said that they came in this lifetime to learn to give love. The goal was not to be with specific people, but rather to learn to love.

"The purpose of my birth was to go down and take some of that cloud peace and light I knew before I was born, and spread it around. To go into the confusion of this society when my preoccupation didn't have to be survival, and to give out love as fully and freely as possible in whatever situation I get into." (Case A-190)

"I feel my purpose in life is to learn to really love as I should." (Case A-200)

"When you asked the purpose, the words 'to get along with others' was repeated three times." (Case A-188)

"I knew that I wanted to be born in order to relieve pain, hurt and sorrow of others. I knew I was given guidance in order to have parents who would help me achieve my purpose." (Case A-251)

"When you asked the purpose, I thought to myself,

'How stupid to wonder what my purpose is. Of course, it's to help people.' " (Case A-333)

"When you asked the purpose, I was aware of many, many lives that I must go through. I will be coming back together with people to work things out. It's like it's not exciting, just something that must be done according to plan. But then it flashed again that the purpose is to work on the universality of all of us and to ease others by talking to them about it. Also it flashed strongly that I must learn not to cling possessively to others." (Case A-360)

"I came into this life to learn love and compassion." (Case A-590)

"I came to this life to become a loving and compassionate being, especially to my husband."
(Case A-586)

"I always felt I was born to the wrong parents, and I questioned the fact of adoption. Now I think I am coming into the real purpose of my life. I have such a compassionate feeling toward other people, and this is something that came to me very strongly when you asked a purpose for this lifetime." (Case A-574)

"My purpose flashed in my mind that I was reborn to learn and grow, to love and to evolve."
(Case A-547)

"My purpose in this lifetime is to learn patience and love of my fellow man, and to relieve loneliness by mixing with other people, and showing compassion."
(Case A-57)

"My purpose for this lifetime was to learn to love and to give, as well as to experience being a female."
(Case A-22)

"My purpose for this lifetime? Simply to love."
(Case A-61)

"My purpose is to learn to love." (Case B-86)

"When you asked the purpose for this lifetime, I

became aware that it was to be a help and to give strength to other people." (Case A-49)

The largest group of the sample—27 percent—said that the purpose of this lifetime was to grow spiritually and to teach others.

"I think my purpose in this life is to learn humility—that everyone inside is the same—there is no better or worse. To show and teach this." (Case A-434)

"I knew that I was here because it is important for me to help others overcome their programming and learn to love." (Case A-143)

"My purpose is to guide other souls through the age of transition, from material culture to cosmic culture." (Case A-419)

"My purpose is to work with others to develop higher consciousness in this time period." (Case B-56)

"I thought I would be needed to help people in the last half of this century. I needed to counsel people psychologically and help physically as the era changed to higher consciousness." (Case A-7)

"My purpose is to experience the channeling of power and how to create results." (Case A-76)

"I know that my purpose was to be a teacher of universal awareness and love. To help the awareness of togetherness really moving forward in the twentieth century." (Case A-383)

"My purpose is to enlighten, heal and broaden people's minds. This lifetime feels very good and positive for me. I feel a burst of energy and of purpose as this came through to me under the hypnosis." (Case B-2)

"I am here to learn, but also to teach and to help in this period of a transition in history from the religious to the scientific to the spiritual life." (Case B-88)

"My purpose is to further my soul's development and understanding with fellow men, and to reach a more profound religious, spiritual, energized higher state of awareness with others." (Case A-377)

"This has been a very enlightening experience, this hypnosis, as I have had the feeling since my earliest memories that I was here for a reason. The purpose of this lifetime that came through when you asked the question was to teach and to minister to mankind and to work on the development of a greater use of the mind and ultimately teach that." (Case B-9)

"My purpose for this lifetime is to do God's work and help during the transition to the cosmic-awareness age." (Case B-2)

"I felt that this lifetime was chosen to experience abandonment, so that I could learn self-sufficiency. I came in this time because this part of the twentieth century is very good for psychological growth, and I will develop my ability to teach and respond to others in this time period." (Case A-378)

The remaining 12 percent of the sample gave purposes that were not as general as those described above. Some of these purposes are interesting and unique.

"My purpose is to overcome fear!" (Case A-353)

"My purpose is to become free of materialism and to combat negativeness. To combine male and female emotions for control, love and strength." (Case B-25)

"My purpose for this lifetime is to learn humility." (Case A-46)

"My purpose for this lifetime is contact with space brothers, bringing together ideas of Western medicine and Eastern healing." (Case B-5)

"My purpose for this lifetime is to evolve from a me-feeling to a we-feeling, to accept responsibility, not to place any restrictions on other people. I am here in this time period to help with the transition." (Case B-82)

"My purpose for this lifetime is to lead a sect of people. I have a feeling it's somehow political." (Case B-41)

"My purpose for being born was to realize my own inner thoughts and independence. The time period was relevant due to women's liberation because it was a time for women to find strength, influence and independence in a man's world." (Case A-454)

"My purpose for this lifetime is to find my identity, and be someone, predominate over my peers and have people look up to me. I need to learn leadership." (Case A-73)

"When you asked the purpose for this lifetime, it came to me that it was a synthesis of diverse elements of culture and religious experience and my own divergent characteristics. To somehow bring them together and to aid in the increasing awareness of the spiritual element of being." (Case A-14)

"I am very happy to be in this life, and it surprised me that my purpose was to be here for strength and courage." (Case A-196)

In summary, the reasons people chose to experience a lifetime on earth were not specifically to develop their own talents. Instead, the purposes were primarily to learn to relate to others and love without being demanding or possessive. There was a sizeable group— 28 percent—who felt that they had a role in teaching mankind to understand his unity with others and to develop his higher consciousness.

My subjects were nearly unanimous in rejecting any purposes involving increase in wealth, status and power. Their responses indicate that at a subconscious level, the Golden Rule is the basic law of the universe. But apparently this rule—that we should treat others as we would like to be treated—is "enforced" by reincarnation. We *will* be treated as we have treated others; we come back to experience being on the giving as well as receiving end. As soon as we finally learn the lesson that we are creating the realities around us—based on our expectations in this life and circumstances chosen by us to redress wrongs we did in past lives—then there is one more lesson to learn. All of us are part of one giant soul organism, all linked together at the higher levels. Jesus said, "What ye do for the least of them, ye do also for me." And we are linked with Christ as we are linked with a prisoner in death row at San Quentin. We are one. This is the Higher Consciousness.

Karmic Ties from Past Lives

We meet someone for the first time and we are instant friends. We shake hands with a stranger and turn away with an unexplained feeling of dislike. Are we just reacting to such clues to similar tastes as the way the stranger is dressed, the expression on his face? Or does it go deeper; are these feelings echoes from the buried memories of our past lives?

I devised a set of questions to see how my subjects responded to the possibility that people in their lives now were known to them in past lives.

Fully 87 percent of all subjects responding to any of the questions about the birth reported that they had known parents, lovers, relatives and friends who were known to them in past lives. Some had more detailed impressions than others, but there was little doubt that my subjects under hypnosis were aware of how they knew people in their lives now from past lives.

Among the 13 percent who reported no answer to this question, the great majority were resisting the whole birth-experience trip. Even though they answered, "No," to the question, "Did you know your mother-to-be, or father, or other people you will meet in this life?" some of their reports indicated that they did have some awareness about this.

"Someone is urging me into this life, promising to follow me. I do not want to be born." (Case A-598)

"All I could get was a feeling of discontent and foreboding, a feeling of fear." (Case A-596)

"I think it was my father who wanted me to be born. It was hard for me to determine my feelings about being born, because it was like a mental block." (Case A-593)

"I felt unattached and displaced. Like a foreign entity in a strange place when I was born." (Case A-585)

Among the 87 percent responding "Yes" to the question about knowing parents in past lives, there was an astonishing variety in the relationships reported. Fathers in this lifetime had been lovers in the past, mothers in the past, brothers, sisters, friends and children. Mothers in the current lifetime were seen as friends, fathers, brothers, sisters, children. There was no consistency at all in the way in which people in this life were related in past lives. The Freudian hypothesis of daughters wishing that fathers were lovers was not evident in the data, nor did sons see their mothers as wives in past lives more frequently than seeing them in other relationships. Often parents in this life were friends or distant relatives in past lives.

Mates and lovers were perceived as friends, close relations, parents from past lives as well as lovers. Some subjects did report that husbands or wives in this lifetime had been in a sexual relationship with them in past lives as well, so there appeared to be a trend for people to work out sexual relationships by assuming the same sex roles in several lifetimes. But again, this was well under one third of the reports of relationships in past lives to husbands or lovers now.

The cases described below show some of the diversity of impressions my subjects had regarding their relationships in past lives with people they know today.

"I knew that my mother was a fellow student at one time, and we had had a very happy companionship. My father was once my older brother who was dull. It seems we made fun of his dullness in a previous life. My grandfather was present at my birth, as he was a doctor, although he did not deliver me. I felt overjoyed to see my grandfather, although I didn't know whether I knew him from a previous existence." (Case A-203)

"I knew from past lives my mother, two friends, and my youngest brother. My mother was my servant, and my father was a lover in past lives. The rest I knew, but not how I knew them. I chose to be a girl because my mother needed a girl." (Case A-508)

"My mother was a mother of mine in a past life and also a child of mine in a past life. My children told me they wanted to be my children before I was born, and I knew them not only from past lives, but from the between-life period." (Case A-381)

"My mother was a sister or close relation in a past life. My father was a captain of a ship I was a sailor on. I got the impression that many other people who were in this life were in one particular lifetime of mine in the 1600's." (Case A-558)

"I noticed a strong physical energy in my heart when you asked about whether I knew my mother, and I had a strong impression she was my sister in a past life." (Case A-91)

"Yes, my mother was an Irish priest in a lifetime I lived with her before. My sister was a nun in the previous life. Both were s.o.b.'s. My father was an

American Indian—a free spirit. I knew that I would experience rejection by my mother and sister." (Case A-338)

"I knew my mother, and I knew I chose her because we had not finished whatever it was we had to work out with each other. I saw one of my friend's daughters in flashbacks of past lives. I knew that she would help me at various times in this life. This is surprising because I don't know this daughter very well now." (Case A-341)

"I knew my mother had been my mother previously. I had been twins with my father, so we were very close. I was aware of numerous other family relationships that stem from past lives. I was glad to be a sister rather than a wife to my brother." (Case A-513)

"My mother was a man for a moment on the table in the operating room, when I was born. She had been a former lover of mine in another life when I was a woman. She was larger than her normal self and had darker hair. I saw my father as a young man, but I could not place the lifetime where I knew him." (Case A-155)

"I did not know my mother, but I knew my father. I seem to have disagreed with my father's choice of a wife until he explained how much she needed us." (Case A-431)

"This was a strange experience. Someone named Louis and I wanted to go together. This was against the advice of the elders, but we were together and felt as though we could change the world. Louis is a twin who left the womb early because he had other things to do, and I was growing in the fetus and Louis wasn't, and I was aware that he was leaving me. I felt distant when I was born and didn't want to be close to other people. I was in a world of strangers and lost without Louis. I got the feeling that Louis' spirit may be helping me now." (Case A-588)

"I became aware that in one of my previous lives my mother killed both my father and myself. Neither she nor my father remember, I became aware, but somehow I always dreamed about this experience. Only now, as I see the relationships here in the hypnosis, have I freed myself." (Case A-589)

"I think I knew my mother before, but it wasn't very clear. What did come through clearly is that an aunt of mine was the person I came to be near, and that she was part of my mother's family. This was the strongest impression of the whole birth experience— the need to be near my aunt whom I knew well in a past life." (Case A-1)

"I had the feeling I was consulting with others I would be born with, and that I had known them in past lives as well. I knew my brother before as a good friend. And there was a friend named June. I wanted her to come too, but she said, "Not this time." I knew my mother and father-to-be, but this wasn't very clear. I know that my daughter's first unborn child will be an old friend." (Case A-191)

"I was aware that my brother from a past life was helping me choose to be born and is my boyfriend in this life. My sister was also there between lives and some other person. I also knew my father before. I was surprised at the experience in the between-life state, recognizing people was amazing on my part!" (Case A-354)

"My mother was a nun in a former life and my father was a gambler. I picked them to experience extremes and help them work out their destiny as well as my own. I felt the purpose of my life was to bring together elements from former lives." (Case A-361)

"I knew my mother before because we had been together at a convent in the 1200's. I saw a close friend of mine as a teenager in Russia, where I knew him." (Case B-71)

"I got no pictures about my mother, but I sensed my father and I have been working on this relationship in several past lives, and we have still not cleaned it up." (Case A-379)

"I knew my mother before when we were both males, and she was a close friend and comrade. I knew my father before, and I had resentment feelings toward him. My son had a close relationship to me in several past lives. It is interesting that I saw my sister as someone that I knew well in the between-life period." (Case A-511)

"Yes, my mother had been my sister, my father and my child before. I saw many people I would know in this life, some of them I have not met yet." (Case A-143)

"My mother was a close male friend from a past life. My father was my wife whom I used to treat cruelly in a past life." (Case A-460)

"I knew my mother in the pre-born state, but not as someone I recognized from a past earth life. My father once caused my death in a past life." (Case A-424)

"My daughter seemed to be someone I was trying desperately to save in a past life. My husband was someone I disliked and feared in a past life." (Case A-328)

"My mother was my mother in a lifetime in 500 B.C. and I didn't necessarily like her then either." (Case A-398)

"My mother was my sister in a past life and my father was a lover. My first son had been a grandfather in one lifetime of mine, my second son had been a father, and my first daughter a friend. My second daughter I saw clearly as a mother of mine in a past life." (Case A-225)

"Yes, I knew my mother from many past lifetimes as friends, sister, and in other relationships. My father was a brother. The people I was with when I was deciding to be born, I knew I would be meeting up with in the future. Some would help guide me from the other states and not be born in my time period." (Case A-372)

In summary, then, 87 percent of all my subjects reported being aware of how they had known important people in their current life from past lives. These relationships were quite varied. Most interesting was the fact that the relationships are not just from past lives, but from the state between lives. This was surprising to my subjects, as indeed it was surprising to me.

My subjects all tell the same story. We come back with the same souls, but in different relationships. We live again not only with those we love, but with those we hate and fear. Only when we feel only compassion and affection are we freed from the need to live over and over with the same spirits, who are also forced to live with us!

VI

WHEN DOES THE SOUL ENTER THE FETUS? IS THE SOUL OF THE INFANT AWARE OF THE FEELINGS OF THE MOTHER?

Is abortion an immoral act, the taking of a human life? This is one of the most hotly debated topics today as our cultural taboos shift and change.

There is no doubt that in almost all human tribes we know about, today and in man's past, the taking of a life within the tribe is taboo. For outsiders, other tribes, the taboo against murder is lifted. War is permissible, for the victims are not tribal members. It is especially taboo to kill the fetus or the newborn, as the tribe welcomes increase in its membership.

But is the fetus a human soul? Is it a soul from conception, or does it become a soul after the fourth month, when its kicks inside the womb signal the mother that there is life inside her?

The response of my subjects to the question: "When does your soul enter the fetus?" provides an interesting answer to this question.

My subjects were perhaps more pro-abortion, as a group, than a cross-section of the American public would be. Yet among the 750 subjects were some practicing Catholics, many Christians, and others who believed that abortion was a form of murder. Yet the 750 subjects were nearly unanimous on one key point.

They felt that the fetus was not truly a part of their consciousness. They existed, fully conscious, as an entity apart from the fetus. Indeed they frequently reported that the fetal body was confining and restrictive, and that they preferred the freedom of out-of-body existence. It was with much reluctance that many of them joined their consciousness with the cellular consciousness of the newborn infant.

When all the 750 cases were analyzed, 89 percent of all the subjects responding said that they did not become a part of the fetus or involved with the fetus until after six months of gestation. Even then, many subjects reported being "in and out" of the fetal body. They viewed themselves as an adult consciousness relating to the fetal body as a less-developed form of life.

Nearly all subjects reported being aware, presumably telepathically, of their mother's emotions before and during their birth.

The largest group in the sample, 33 percent, said that they did not join the fetus, or experience inside the fetus, until just before or during the birth process.

"When you asked about my attachment to the fetus, I was outside waiting for it to be ready for birth, so that I could enter. When you asked about the feelings of my mother, I became aware that she was nervous and not too happy about the birth." (Case A-525)

"I attached to the fetus somewhere toward the end of the ninth month. When you asked about the emotions of my mother just before birth, I got the sensation that she was indifferent. Strange—I became aware that she was discussing financial worries with my father. I could not get a clear impression of where I was before birth. I seemed to be confused and felt as if I was somehow being nagged to join this fetus and live this lifetime." (Case A-498)

"I attached to the fetus just before birth. When you asked about my mother, I had the feeling being pregnant was a nuisance to her, and a feeling that was partially why I wasn't attached to the fetus earlier because it wasn't very pleasant." (Case A-444)

"I was not completely attached to the fetus, and I was able to be, and to move, as before I entered the fetus. I only came when it was ready to be born. I was aware of my mother's emotion. She was afraid, and I also became aware of the doctor and the nurses, and aware of the delivery room." (Case A-426)

"When you asked about attachment to the fetus, I became somewhat frightened by its growth. I became aware the fetus was getting bigger and closer to birth, but I remain outside until birth. But there's confusion as to when that "moment" of joining is. When you asked the emotions of my mother just before birth, I became aware I posed a very problematic birth, and it was a problem for her. She blamed me, and so hated me somewhat for not 'doing it' properly." (Case A-420)

"I seemed unattached to the fetus until the moment of birth, and I did not see the fetus clearly. When you asked the feelings of my mother, I became aware that she did not want to have another child and did not want to go through with the birth, but I knew this was all unconscious on her part." (Case A-330)

"I came in at the beginning for a while, while the fetus was developing, but I split when it got too squishy, and didn't come back until just before it was time for me to be born. When you asked the emotions of my mother just before and during birth, I felt that she was unaware of me when I was born because she had been sedated. I get sadness and fear feelings from her. She is afraid of aloneness upon my arrival." (Case A-313)

"I attached to the fetus near the moment when the birthing process begins. I was aware of my mother's feelings, and I realized the profundity of her feelings of motherhood. She was 'out' during birth, and I felt alienated from her because of this." (Case A-284)

"When you asked about the attachment to the fetus, a vivid image and feeling came to me. I seemed to be positioned with my head toward my mother's opening and I felt my shoulders in blood. When you asked the emotions of my mother, I had a "heavy" sensation. I seemed to know she was glad about my birth, but sorry about the extra burden I would pose. I didn't realize the sadness and unhappiness involved in this until this hypnosis session." (Case A-238)

"When you asked about the attachment to the fetus, it felt like I was floating above the delivery table until the birth. I was attached by a cord. But I was aware that my mother was very loving and eager to receive me." (Case A-224)

(This subject is a twin.) "Shortly before birth we entered the fetuses. We were fighting about which body to pick, the blonde or the brown-haired fetus. I was aware of my mother's emotions. She was happy, but she was ready to unload." (Case A-153)

"When you asked about attachment to the fetus, I had none. It seems that I just observed it. I was aware of the emotions of my mother. I was being counseled up to the time I entered the body." (Case A-123)

"I wasn't attached to the fetus until I heard some voices (I think they were my guides who helped me choose to be born) warn me that the birth would be premature and they urged me to "hurry up and get in there" at about seven months. When you asked the emotions of my mother, I felt extreme fear on her part." (Case A-98)

"I attached to the fetus just before birth. When you asked the emotions of my mother, I felt that either she or I had a strong sensation in the heart area, an 'emotional hurt' sensation." (Case A-84)

"When you asked about the attachment to the fetus, I thought: 'Attachment?' I felt it was a focus that was building in intensity, and my broad self gradually focused into it, like funneled into it. And as I tunneled in more and more until birth, my ties outside of physical reality diminished and it just sort of left me here in this world. When you asked the emotions of my mother, I was aware in a broad sense but not specifically. I was more aware just of her energy." (Case A-101)

"When you asked about the attachment to the fetus, I felt I was in and out of it. I joined it at three months but wouldn't be there all the time. I was mainly interested in what my mother and father to be were like. When you asked the emotions of my mother, I felt that she was nervous, but not unduly so. I knew she wanted me to be special and that everything should be right for me. Strange, I became aware that she was mad at the doctor for being late." (Case A-351)

"I feel certain that I did not enter the fetus until the last minute. I was too happy and too busy elsewhere. I was not interested at all in spending time in the fetus. When you asked the emotions of my mother, I became aware that she felt mildly resigned and somewhat happy and proud. It was more something she had to do than wanted to do. She did not mind being pregnant, it was okay." (Case A-490)

"I attached to the fetus when it was almost out of the birth canal. I suddenly felt a choking sensation, pain, anguish. I felt that my mother was frightened and rather ambivalent about having a baby." (Case A-489)

"I came into the fetus immediately before birth, and I did experience the total birth in the fetus. When you asked about my mother, I became vividly aware that she was utterly terrified and quivery. She didn't dare say anything to my father or the doctor. She was very scared, and that's part of why I was present during birth. The feeling I had was that the fetus would have survived if I hadn't joined consciousness with it earlier than I had planned, but when I became aware of my mother's great fear, it seemed important that I be there." (Case A-393)

"When you asked about the fetus, I became aware that I was looking at it. I then joined it before birth. When I did join it I felt a choking sensation, and felt that I was choked by the umbilical cord at birth." (Case A-487)

"I delayed in my attachment to the fetus, and I just barely made it in as contractions started. When you asked about the feelings of my mother, I had strong feelings of her sensations in the stomach, vibrating through me." (Case B-63)

"I attached to the fetus just before birth, and then I left during birth and rejoined it as soon as I took my first breath. I became aware that my mother cried a lot and didn't really want me." (Case A-486)

Twenty percent of my subjects reporting their attachment to the fetus said that they were outside the fetus, without specifying that they joined just before birth. These subjects often seemed resistant to being born.

"I was not in the fetus, but I felt very close to my mother. I became aware that she loved me and wanted me to come." (Case A-541)

"When you asked about attachment to the fetus, I became aware that I was outside circling around it. I knew that my mother was quite frightened." (Case A-404)

"I mostly observed the fetus, but at one point I felt a pulsating sensation around my body. I don't know whether this was because I was in the fetus, but it was a sensation I had. I feel that I really observed the fetus. When you asked the emotions of my mother, it came through vividly. She felt very intense fear and also regret." (Case A-390)

"I was outside the fetus, and I could see the problem of my birth, that I was a breech delivery. So I didn't join until later. I became aware of my mother's great fear." (Case A-366)

"When you asked about my attachment to the fetus, I saw it rather than being inside it. I see the fetus curled, almost holding the long umbilical cord which was shortened into the shape of a writer's pen, which is my purpose in life. This imagery seemed to be a way of expressing the fact that I was outside the fetus thinking about my purpose before I was born. When you asked the emotions of my mother, I became aware that she was ambivalent about losing me from her womb, and therefore she did not push as well as she could have." (Case A-324)

"When you asked about attachment to the fetus, I felt that I was not attached to the fetus but instead hovered around my mother. When you asked the emotions of my mother, I didn't get emotions, but I saw her with a pregnant belly." (Case A-252)

"When you asked about the attachment to the fetus, I felt as though my region of movement was restricted to a certain radius around my mother, which grew smaller as the day of birth approached. When you asked the feelings of my mother, I sensed a strong desire to get me out and felt rejection." (Case A-170)

"I seemed to be hanging around the fetus, admiring it, wanting to join it, but I didn't do so until birth. When you asked the emotions of my mother I became aware that they were negative. She was not happy and she did not accept her situation." (Case A-206)

"When you asked about my attachment to the fetus, I wasn't attached at all. I was outside. I felt fond of it and protective of it. I didn't get any reaction to your question about the emotions of my mother." (Case A-385)

"I just observed the fetus from a distance and did not join it. I tried not to be aware of the emotions of my mother and got no impressions from this." (Case A-293)

"I was outside the fetus. I watched in amazement at this form developing, knowing it would become mine, protecting it with my own energy as well as my mother's. When you asked about the emotion of my mother, I felt anger, distress, coldness and a great deal of fear and pain. There was a convulsing feeling, crying, and then I blacked out." (Case A-348)

"I wasn't attached to the fetus, but I seemed somehow to be next to it. I was aware of the emotions of my mother, and I sensed that she felt great fear and was weak. I seemed to know this meant I would have fear in my life." (Case A-482)

"When asked about attachment to the fetus, I had an impersonal feeling, like I was waiting for a new home to be completed. I wasn't aware of the emotions

of my mother. I seemed to want to remain detached."
(Case A-382)

"Instead of being in the fetus, I stayed in front of
my mother around her uterus, but not in her body. I
was aware that she was excited and happy." (Case
A-372)

"I was not attached to the fetus, and I felt displaced, as well as unattached. I was aware that my
mother felt agony, pain, joy and apprehension." (Case
A-585)

Another 19 percent of the sample described themselves as being in and out of the fetus during the
period before birth.

"I was mostly out of the fetus' body. At one point
I saw a cross-section of my mother with the fetus
inside. Then I pictured my mother in the bed and
bedroom that they had when I was born. I hadn't
known that I was aware of this bedroom and the
furniture in it. When you asked about the emotions of
my mother, she was tired of waiting and tired of having to stay in bed to avoid a miscarriage. There were
some misgivings about pregnancy, but this was the
second time so she was more relaxed." (Case A-520)

"I seemed to be in and out of the fetus to check on
development. After birth I stayed with the baby more,
but I still could leave the body. I was aware that my
mother was quite anxious and afraid for my health
just before and during birth." (Case A-510)

"When you asked about the attachment to the fetus,
I felt that I was just interested from time to time in
perceiving from the inside, but mostly outside. I
seemed to be adjusting it to fit my awareness. My
only awareness of the feeling of my mother was a
feeling of strong fatigue." (Case A-472)

"It seemed I could both watch and be internalized
in the fetus. I became aware that my right chest hurt

when I was perceiving inside the fetus! Don't know why. When you asked the emotions of my mother, nothing special came to my mind at all." (Case A-471)

"I seemed to be intermittently in and out of the fetus. I felt it was not too safe being out during birth, but I detached somewhat and then was back just after I emerged from the birth canal. When you asked the emotions of my mother before and during birth, I felt that she left *her* body (anesthesia?), and seemed to avoid it." (Case A-356)

"When you asked about the fetus, I saw it and nurtured it and watched out for it, and also was in it all the way a few times, but not most of the time. I came in much more after birth than before birth. When you asked the emotions of my mother, I was clearly aware of them. She was a little sad and upset because of Dad not giving her enough attention, and she was also deeply happy." (Case A-327)

"My attachment to the fetus seemed to be quite tenuous. I was in and out of the fetus when born. I felt awareness of my mother's pain when I was out of the fetus, but not when I was in it." (Case A-257)

"When you asked about the attachment to the fetus, I became aware that I went in and out, but was not firmly attached. I was more aware before birth of being attached to the fetus than during the birth experience. I think I was blocking the pain of the experience and, therefore, blocked a lot of the feeling too. I was aware that my mother didn't really want a child, but was receptive." (Case A-178)

"When you asked about the attachment to the fetus, at first I went in a little and came right back to the 'other place.' I was really in and out. I wasn't aware of the emotions of my mother." (Case A-524)

"When you asked about the attachment to the fetus, I seemed to be going back and forth, in and out alternatively. I viewed the fetus with compassion and anticipation. When you asked the feelings of my mother I had a sense of adoration, and an awareness that we were old friends (this is strange because she doesn't seem so now)." (Case B-14)

"I seemed to go in and out of the fetus and wasn't very interested in it. I seemed to both see the fetus and see from the fetus. My view seemed to be moving up and down, as though I were doubtful about being in the body at all. I wasn't aware of the feeling of my mother." (Case B-94)

"I kept coming and going from the fetus, like I was unsure. I was aware that my mother was quite upset and in deep pain. She didn't want me. I was premature and I get the impression that this was an effort on my part and my mother's because she didn't want me, and I really didn't want to be born." (Case A-261)

"All that happened when you asked about the fetus was that I felt warmth for an instant, and then I was out of the fetus and I saw an image of my mother just before giving birth. I wasn't aware of her feelings." (Case A-81)

"At around five months' pregnancy I began to go in and out of the fetus, but I was not rigidly attached. The feelings of my mother were discomfort." (Case B-23)

"It's interesting when you asked about attachment to the fetus. I seemed to be attached when in the womb, but even as I was not yet physically within it, I seem to be in and out. Everything was bright and I was aware of all physical sensations. When you asked the question about the feelings of my mother, I felt warm and she felt safe and secure." (Case A-17)

"Starting at about five months I was occasionally

going in and coming out. I seemed to be outside looking in most of the time. I didn't have any vivid impressions of my mother's feelings." (Case A-21)

"I don't seem to have too much attachment to the fetus. I'm a little impatient with its growth and am jumping in and out of being in it before birth. I seem to join it more at about eight months. When you asked about the feelings of my mother, she was excited and anxious, it being the first." (Case A-194)

"When you asked the question about attachment to the fetus, it seemed that I came and went. I really didn't get into identifying with it until after birth. I seemed more to be checking to see if it was okay. I was aware that my mother was worried." (Case A-493)

"When the shape is recognizably human, I visit in and out of the fetus. When you asked the feelings of my mother, I feel that she is thinking she must go through with what she began, because it is her duty." (Case A-154)

"When you asked about the attachment to the fetus, it seemed that I checked out its development sporadically. I have a feeling that it was to be a superior being, but there is no emotional attachment to that statement. I think I just wanted to check to make sure the fetus would be fine. When you asked the emotions of my mother, I had a strange sensation that my mother had fully taken on her "humanoid" role. I knew that my mother had worked with me on a previous project, but she was not in touch with that when I was the fetus." (Case A-195)

"I came into the fetus just before birth when it was in trouble, and I had to keep it going. Before that I was in and out. When you asked the feelings of my mother, I felt that she knew I wouldn't die and would make it. She had great joy. (I was born three months premature and was in an incubator for eight weeks.)" (Case A-476)

"When you asked about attachment to the fetus, I was in and out, like it was a game. I had feelings both emotional and physical relating to the fetus, but was not really in it much. I was aware of the feelings of my mother just before my birth: "Oh, my God, it's now!" (Case A-377)

"I seemed to be in and out of the fetus and a period of partial attachment seemed to go on for some months. I had a strange feeling about my mother. I became aware of her organs when I was inside the fetus, and it felt very familiar." (Case B-88)

"I was in and out of the fetus, but when I was in the fetus, I was not aware of my true self. When you asked the emotions of my mother, I had a strong feeling that she was full of fear and hate." (Case A-156)

"I felt some attachment to the fetus, but I was mostly out. I saw the fetus developing, and I felt I was influencing its development. When you asked the feelings of my mother, I felt that she wanted me out." (Case A-73)

"I was in and out of the fetus, and while I was inside my mother I was feeling playful with her and we communicated somehow emotionally. Just before the birth she was feeling deep affection. During the birth she was trying very hard, but she was feeling frightened and lonely." (Case A-462)

"I was in and out of the fetus until the moment of birth. I felt my mother's feelings and knew that she was reluctant and apprehensive. She felt angry and was in great pain." (Case A-143)

"I was in and out of the fetus. Somehow I felt more control inside, because I was very determined to be in this family. I was sure I could make them want me too, if I had a chance. When you asked about the feelings of my mother, she felt, 'Hurry up, I'm weak and tired.'" (Case A-191)

"I was in and out of the fetus, and was rather concerned and hovering around it, but I was seldom in it. I was aware of the feelings of my mother. She was so emotional and frightened, she made me mad. It was a deterrent rather than a help, her excessive emotion." (Case A-513)

"I was in and out of the fetus, and it seemed there were two different worlds, outside and inside the fetus. The attachment is not total. I was very aware of the emotions of my mother, before birth especially." (Case A-102)

"I was in a back-and-forth association with the fetus, mostly just watching myself grow. When you asked the emotions of my mother, I got a strong sensation of a headache." (Case A-246)

"I was in and out of the fetus before birth. Just before birth I became aware that there was something wrong with my mother. She seemed to be out of it. I felt, 'I'll be glad to get out.'" (Case A-356)

Another group of 5 percent of my subjects reported that they did not really enter the fetus even at birth, but were able to leave the fetal consciousness at will after birth.

"I seemed to be hovering over the fetus while it was born. I was not inside the fetus. It took three days to be born, and my mother had had a very hard birth." (Case A-505)

"My attachment to the fetus was quite tenuous. I didn't enter the body until well after birth. When you asked the emotions of my mother, I forgot to look. I feel I could have known them, but didn't wish to." (Case A-483)

"I seemed to be attending to the fetus' growth and

development from in and out. I was quite doting. But even after birth I was not fully in the body. I was aware that my mother was filled with her dreams. Finally, after the birth I locked in. The body and I are locked after the first breath and cry." (Case A-461)

"I was mostly out of the fetus. I was also out a lot until one year of age. I became aware that my mother was uptight and nervous before and during the birth." (Case A-410)

"I was not attached to the fetus until after birth. I was aware of the feelings of my mother. She had a mixture of happiness and resignation to pain and possible death. (My mother was thirty-three and I was the first and only child.)" (Case A-234)

"When you asked about the attachment to the fetus, I became aware that I almost escaped. I ceased to breathe, but was resuscitated and then joined the body. When you asked about the awareness of my mother's emotions, I felt strongly that she felt she owned me." (Case A-167)

"When you asked about the attachment to the fetus, I felt I attached right away after birth, but I didn't like it. I found it hostile in that environment. My next entry seemed to be a few weeks later. I was not aware of the feelings of my mother." (Case B-80)

"I attached to the fetus toward the end of gestation more and more, and then attached right after birth. Even after birth I sometimes faded out. When you asked the feelings of my mother, I felt she had felt confusion, and she was not quite in control or totally into it." (Case A-441)

"I had no attachment to the fetus. I did not enter until the sixth day of physical life. When you asked the emotions of my mother, I became aware that she knew that she would die in two days. I observed all this from a different space." (Case A-383)

"I attached to the fetus directly after birth for a brief moment, and then 'stood guard.' I was aware that my mother felt resentment and some bitterness." (Case A-437)

Twelve percent of my subjects reported being in the fetus after about six months gestation.

"My mother has been my daughter in a past life. I was aware of my desire to send her nurturing energy before I went into her body. I felt very involved in the creation of the baby. I wanted everything to be perfect. I went into the fetus after it was formed completely, in the last month or so of pregnancy. I was aware that my mother wanted to bring me to life, but she was a little worried and nervous." (Case A-492)

"I felt that I joined the fetus at the eighth or ninth month. My consciousness seemed to attach itself to that of the fetus at that time. I knew that my mother felt joy and expectation before the birth, but she was under anesthesia during the birth, and I lost any awareness of her feelings because of that." (Case A-400)

"I was in the fetus for a while before birth. It felt warm and safe. I wasn't looking forward to birth. When you asked the emotions of my mother, I became aware that we are preparing to confront one another." (Case A-370)

"At the age of six months' gestation, I seemed to have a strong attachment to the fetus. I felt some resentment from my mother, but I also feel very safe with her in spite of her grumblings." (Case A-309)

"I don't really know when I joined the consciousness of the fetus. When I joined it was dark, and I couldn't wait to get out. I became aware that my mother was arguing with my father and I felt her love and gentleness at another time." (Case A-211)

"It seemed that I attached to the fetus somewhere around a month before birth. I know it wasn't long before birth. When you asked the emotions of my mother, I was aware of them before I was born. She had been a friend in a past life, so we had rapport." (Case A-231)

"I seemed to attach to the fetus, or become aware of it, around the sixth month of gestation. I wasn't aware of the feelings of my mother during the birth experience, but earlier, before I joined the fetus, I felt great anger from her." (Case A-549)

"It seemed to me that I was outside the fetus until six or eight months. My mother did not want me, and we were both angry. I seemed to be aware of this before birth." (Case A-412)

"I seemed to wait until the fetus was almost complete before I entered it. My mother has mixed feelings. She's not sure she has made the right choice." (Case A-136)

"It seemed that I entered the fetus at six months, and I stayed but intermittently. I'm out of it also. I became aware that my mother was angry and frightened, and kept wanting to get rid of me. I communicated to her to allow me to live." (Case A-493)

"I seemed to attach to the fetus after it was more developed, at six months or so, but I still went in and out. My mother had much tension just before my birth, then some kind of arousal, and then I felt her release." (Case A-345)

"I seemed to join the fetus about six months. Before that it was more like animal or plant life. My mother's feelings seemed to be contentment." (Case B-81)

"I seemed to attach at the fetus about six months'

gestation. I was aware of my mother's feelings, I knew she was afraid of yelling out during the birth experience." (Case A-36)

"I seemed to be aware in the fetus at about eight months of age. I knew that my mother wanted a girl. Interestingly, I also got some suppressed emotions from her regarding my father at this time." (Case A-413)

"I seemed to attach to the fetus when the fetus was fully formed—somewhere in the last trimester. I felt warmth from my mother's body, and then I became aware of her fear of birth." (Case B-19)

"I attached to the fetus sometime in late pregnancy. I felt the tension of my mother's body, and her state of being nervous and unhappy. I was aware that she felt resentment at carrying me and fear of the birth." (Case A-22)

"I seem to attach to the fetus somewhere midway in pregnancy, closer to the end. I was aware that my mother was scared initially, then accepted the natural process. I felt two heartbeats almost through the entire birth experience." (Case A-200)

"I got inside the fetus toward the end (last couple of months). I liked the feeling of a womb, warm and secure. When you asked the emotions of my mother, I did seem to know them. She did not want me. She tried to abort me once and was angry at my birth because she wanted to divorce my father. I realize now that part of my karma this time is to be aware of my mother's feelings toward me and to learn to love her anyway. I could really have gotten into crying immediately after my birth." (Case A-242)

"I seemed to attach to the fetus around seven months, but it was not a strong attachment. I became aware that my mother was angry at my father." (Case A-287)

Only 11 percent of the sample reported being aware of being inside the fetus any time between conception and the six-month gestation period. This is interesting, as all my subjects were aware that the first kick occurs in the fourth month of pregnancy. In spite of this objective knowledge, only 11 percent of all the subjects perceived themselves as inside the fetus when these "signs of life" arise.

"It seemed to me that I attached after the fetus was well formed, and it was warm and cozy in the womb. I felt my mother's excitement before birth. It was a tingly feeling that was transmitted to me. I got no response from her at the birth, because she was asleep." (Case A-375)

"It seemed to me that I experienced the individual cells of the fetus first, and then the body as a whole from the inside. The emotions of my mother just before birth were that she was excited when it begins. Beyond that I don't know because I'm busy." (Case A-374)

"It seemed that I attached at the moment of conception, even though I knew it was going to be a fairly boring nine months and was eager to be born. I was aware that my mother was anxious and a little nervous and frightened." (Case A-305)

"It seemed to me that I came early into the fetus, at about five months. My mother seemed hysterical, and I was also hysterical and screaming just before birth and during." (Case A-269)

"Yes, I attached to the fetus, but I don't know when. In the fetus I felt very warm when I heard the da-dum, da-dum heartbeat." (Case A-118)

"It seemed that I joined when the fetus is in a very primitive state with the fingers still webbed. I had a long wait in there! I was aware that my mother felt happy and peaceful, although a little scared at the beginning of labor." (Case A-208)

"It seemed when you asked about my attachment to the fetus that I was a fish—fetus, making constant rounds in the womb. I seemed to be playing. My mother was quite calm and happy." (Case A-339)

"I feel that the fetus was probably three or four months old when I became aware of it. The heartbeat of the fetus is pulsating at this time. I was aware of the feelings of my mother quite clearly." (Case A-576)

"I seemed to attach to the fetus between the flipper stage and before the development of eyes. I became aware that my mother was anxious and aggravated, pacing back and forth." (Case B-37)

"I seemed to attach to the fetus at conception. I was aware that my mother wanted to atone for the death of my brother." (Case A-310)

"When you asked the question about attachment to the fetus, I felt I was very dependent and I stay in all the time. My mother seemed calm, accepting, secure." (Case A-199)

"It seemed to me that I surrounded the fetus until it developed a heartbeat, then I entered it. My feelings of my mother were ones of happiness and relief and awe at the birth experience. In some ways the impressions I got under hypnosis seemed sort of made up, except for my involvement with the fetus. This came through strongly." (Case B-69)

"I felt I attached to the fetus, became aware of it, at the moment of conception. My mother had some pain, but she was also happy." (Case A-213)

"It seemed that I attached to the fetus somewhere around three months of gestation. I felt strong dislike coming to me from my mother, she didn't want me." (Case B-70)

"When you asked about my attachment to the fetus, it flashed in my mind that it was third week, first day. The feelings of my mother were mixed. She wanted me very much, but I became aware that she was afraid of being inadequate as a mother." (Case B-5)

"It seemed I attached to the fetus at about eight weeks. When you asked a question about the emotions of my mother, I was aware of a connection between us and a great affinity. But I have no direct recall of her emotions." (Case A-91)

Five percent of the cases could not be classified in terms of when they attached to the fetus. Because some of these are quite interesting, I am quoting many of these cases.

"When you asked the time of attachment to the fetus, all I got were feelings of warmth and vagueness that I can't really describe. I wasn't aware of the feelings of my mother." (Case A-523)

"When you asked about attachment to the fetus, what came through clearly was that I left during the birth process because of all the drugs and anesthesia. I felt my mother was anxious." (Case A-522)

"Attachment to the fetus felt like floating, it was a very nice feeling, self-contained. My mother was fearful and unsure. I came early so she would not worry, and to make it easier for her." (Case A-422)

"I felt safe and secure in the fetus and didn't want to leave. I was aware of my mother's fear." (Case A-401)

"I seemed to be inside the fetus, in the hands. I was experiencing from this point. My feelings were that she was a bit nervous but under control, and she really felt confident." (Case A-255)

"I wanted to stay there in the fetus with the placenta. I was hugging it and wanted to be with it.

From my mother I got a feeling of anxiety." (Case A-168)

"My attachment to the fetus was interesting. It was as if it was in anticipation, gradually requiring more juice and acceptance of new rigor. I was aware that my mother was loaded with apprehension regarding her ability to be a mother, and had lots of fears and guilt." (Case A-127)

"It seemed that my mother and I were the same until the consciousness entered the fetus, at which point we separated, with me remaining essentially unchanged, and she changing a great deal. I seemed to be in control, and she felt helpless. This was all very confusing." (Case A-117)

"The attachment to the fetus seemed earlier than I had consciously thought. I knew my mother wanted to commit suicide when she found herself pregnant with me, but this experience tells me she had come to a not too unpleasant kind of resignation. She was quite fearful generally." (Case A-140)

"When you asked about my attachment to the fetus, I suddenly flashed on being very uncomfortable and cramped. I was back in prison. Negative sensations. I was aware under the hypnosis that my mother did not want the pregnancy and had much mental turmoil with physical and emotional trauma." (Case A-582)

"I did seem to be attached to the fetus, but all that came was that I seemed shrimp-like, a sea creature in a translucent stage. The uterus is glowing red like the inside of a flower." (Case B-74)

"I felt that the fetus was almost something totally separate until I became this being. I felt hesitance and fear from my mother." (Case A-315)

"When you asked about attachment to the fetus, it seemed like it was almost prior to conception and it was much the same as the attachment to my present body. I knew my mother was hoping for a son to replace one she lost." (Case B-17)

"I attached to the fetus when I first saw my toes, and they were warm, reddish-orange, against a black wall. I wasn't aware of the feelings of my mother." (Case B-64)

"I was inside the fetus, and I got a kind of "vortex" feeling and was later aware of a cramped position. I tried not to be aware of the feelings of my mother." (Case A-99)

"When you asked the attachment to the fetus, I saw myself looking at it and then being in it with a strong feeling of no turning back. I was aware that my mother was happy." (Case A-593)

In summary, 89 percent of my subjects expressed the feeling that their consciousness was something separate from that of the fetus, and they did not experience inside the fetus to any degree until at least the sixth month. A majority of the subjects did not experience the fetus until just before birth. Of those who reported joining the fetus from conception to four months, their description indicated they might have also been experiencing in and out of the fetus.

Eighty-six percent of all the subjects said that they became aware of the feelings, emotions and even thoughts of their mother before they were born. Many of the subjects said that they were aware of the mother's feelings because they themselves were not locked into the fetus, but instead seemed to be hovering around it.

Fourteen percent of the subjects said that they either did not get any impression of the mother's feelings, or blocked it from awareness because of their general resistance to being born. Many subjects ex-

WHEN DOES THE SOUL ENTER THE FETUS? 121

pressed surprise at becoming aware of their mother's feelings under this hypnotic state.

What light does this study shed on the question of abortion? One impression that emerges from these 750 cases is that birth—and indeed living another lifetime—is perceived as a duty and not a pleasure. The soul apparently has a choice of which fetus to enter. If one fetus is aborted, apparently it is possible to choose another.

In some cases, the soul who will occupy the fetus is in contact with the soul of the mother and can influence her decision regarding abortion. My data also indicates that souls can elect to leave the fetus or the infant's body and return to the between-life state. Perhaps the sudden death syndrome in infants may be the result of a soul's decision not to go ahead with a life plan.

VII

TAKING THE BIG STEP—
GETTING BORN

My subjects had some interesting experiences in moving down the birth canal, emerging into the world and becoming aware of their environment. My attempts to statistically analyze the actual birth were met with frustration. Each person seemed to express the experience slightly differently. The one solid statistic I gathered was that 16 percent of my subjects chose not to experience the actual physical birth, in response to my instructions that they could avoid it if they wished. This meant that 84 percent of my subjects did go through the birth process under the hypnosis. I had suggested that they would feel no pain, but in spite of this suggestion, several subjects did experience specific discomforts. Some of them reported that they didn't feel actual pain, but were aware of portions of their body where there was trouble during the birth experience, and also experienced other sensations relating to birth.

Most impressive in the reports was the degree of sadness experienced about emerging into the world.

Even though for many of my subjects the actual birth was not physically traumatic, a sense of sorrow pervaded the experience. At least 10 percent of the subjects said that they felt sad, or actually cried tears during the birth experience. The feelings of sadness seemed to be on emerging from the womb. This is a most interesting finding. It may be that regressions to the birth experience to remove neurotic fears, as practiced by Arthur Janov of primal-scream-therapy fame, relate not so much to the actual birth as to the experience of being "caught" or trapped in a physical body after the freedom of the between-life experience.

Many subjects reported that the onrush of physical sensations on emerging from the birth canal was disturbing and very unpleasant. Apparently the soul exists in a quite different environment in the between-life state. The physical senses bring so much vivid input that the soul feels almost "drowned" in light, cold air, sounds. Surprising to me was the frequent report that the soul in the new-born infant feels cut off, diminished, alone compared to the between-life state. To be alive in a body is to be alone and unconnected. Perhaps we are alive to learn to break through the screen of the senses, to experience while in a body the transcendent self we truly are.

But I will let my subjects speak for themselves. I will report many of the birth experiences as they were written by my subjects on their data sheets, so that the reader can get a clearer notion of the variety and flavor of the actual birth experience under hypnosis.

"When you asked about the birth-canal experience, I was aware that it was a hot day in July, too hot to put forth the energy to be born. I was pushed out anyway. I wanted to wait a few days. I saw and felt my father's hands after I was born and also felt the heat. I felt strongly that I couldn't breathe. My father was feeling frantic, but his hands were adept. He made me breathe. I already knew I was born on a hot July day, delivered by my father. As birth began, my body in the here-and-now hypnosis began to perspire." (Case A-528)

"The birth canal experience for me was a tight struggle, and my first experience out of the birth canal was a bright light which made me mad, like someone switching the light on when you're sleeping. I was angry as soon as I was born, and I felt resentment from the people in the delivery room, but not my mother." (Case A-526)

"The birth-canal experience for me was curiously different. I was amazed by the light when I emerge and I'm very chilly. I cried. They take me away from Mom, and I'm terrified, then I realized they care and that they will give me back to Mom. I was aware that the people in the delivery room were caring, even though they didn't understand me." (Case A-371)

"In the birth canal I felt stifled. I felt tight and uncomfortable. As soon as I emerged from the canal I can breathe, and the first breath was wonderful. I got feelings of great happiness and relief from others in the delivery room. I feel great loving hands and stroking and soft voices. This experience was very clear. I felt 'love' in the room. I wonder if it was because my family was in the room. My grandfather delivered me." (Case A-16)

"The birth-canal experience for me was impatience, a realization that tolerance would be a major stumbling block for me in this life. As soon as I was born I felt intense cold and bright light. I was afraid of the prospects ahead of me. I felt that the doctors and nurses in attendance were impersonal and cold. They lacked compassion for my mother's fear and pain. I recall being very upset by this lack of feeling of those in attendance. I hovered over my mother throughout this ordeal." (Case A-485)

"The birth-canal experience for me was terrifying. It was so shaky, like an earthquake. I had feelings of claustrophobia and suffocation. As soon as I emerged, I felt blinding light. There were too many impressions and I felt overwhelmed, too exposed. I felt lost in space. I wasn't aware of other people in the delivery room. The birth was very scary for me as well as physically painful. There is a terrible sense of being lost in space with nothing to comfort me or enfold me." (Case A-468)

"In the birth-canal experience I feel strong pressure on my head, and I was thinking, 'We can do it!' Then I start to feel sad. As soon as I emerged from the birth canal, I felt extreme sadness. I am crying. I am too freaked out by the strong stimuli to be very aware. It was hard to know if the feelings I felt were my feelings or those of the others in the delivery room. I feel so sad that I am so alone and my life will be so hard." (Case A-452)

"The birth experience for me was moving from a large space into a narrow space. After birth I saw the very bright lights which hurt my eyes. I had a sense of spaciousness. I feel calm, but my mother is hysterical, demanding attention from the doctors and nurses. I am watching the scene with cool detachment." (Case A-448)

"My birth-canal experience started with a strong feeling that somehow 'they' tricked me. They induced the labor and I wasn't ready yet. My feelings after birth were, 'Oh well, here I am. I'll give it another go.' I was aware that there was jealousy on my older brother's part, and also that everyone was unhappy with my sex. It wasn't a very pleasant introduction to the world." (Case A-446)

"When you asked about the birth-canal experience, I don't think I felt anything, but I got the feeling I was going out, but didn't have any physical feeling. But then as I emerged from the birth canal I could taste blood, and I think the forceps twisted my head so that my neck got pinched. I had a real bummer of a headache because there were lots of bright, bright lights. There was lots of activity in the delivery room after I was born, because I think my head was dented." (Case A-428)

"I didn't have a birth-canal experience because I joined just as the baby was delivered. I felt cramped at first, then wondered, 'How do I communicate with these people?' I felt I observed at least a general visual image of the delivery room, but I still felt a little detached from the new baby. But I went on with it anyway." (Case A-414)

"In the birth canal I felt tight and very constricted and I was aware of darkness. As soon as I emerged I saw very bright lights and heard loud noises. As soon as I was born I was aware of other people's feelings. I was surprised to find that my mother didn't want me. People were impersonal. I think to myself, 'This is going to be a lonely trip.' I think I must have rushed into this life." (Case A-406. This subject felt very eager to be born and was quite excited about the prospect. Apparently, once she was born she felt that she had made a bad choice.)

"The birth-canal experience felt like an earthquake with everything moving, pulsating, exploding—I was aware of speed and panic feelings. My impressions after birth were intense fear. I was aware of other people's feelings in the delivery room. There were a doctor and two nurses. The doctor had a bit of feeling of wonder at the miracle of birth, but the nurses were just doing a job and were glad it was over. My mother was relieved, drugged, tired." (Case A-500)

"The birth-canal experience was strange. I feel my face was mashed down and my arms were pushed close to my chest. When I emerged I was cold and the room was cold. It pissed me off to be cold and held away from Mother in the lights. I was aware that my dad was awed and worried, but he seemed to be moved and quiet. My mother was nervous and talky and then became groggy. The doctor seemed nonchalant, but he was also kind." (Case B-51)

"When you asked about the birth-canal experience, I had a feeling of fighting, like I hadn't argued or put up a fight until the actual experience, because I kept hoping it wouldn't happen. My impressions after birth were that I was in a vast area, and I felt lost and very cold." (Case A-457. This subject couldn't decide whether or not to be born.)

"During the birth-canal experience, my back began to ache. I felt as though I were flexing, and I felt angry about this. Right after birth, I felt things were very funny. My feeling was that the people in the delivery room know nothing, and you know it all. And this struck me as being cosmically funny." (Case B-59)

"My birth-canal experience was unpleasant, and the feelings were strong that I wished I weren't being born. I want to change my mind. My sensory impressions after I was born were of confusion and sadness and the lack of warmth around me. My mother seemed very sad and my father felt guilty. The whole feeling of birth seemed to be an annoying, unpleasant 'trip' to accomplish something in this lifetime. I feel an urgency." (Case A-408)

"My birth-canal experience was that I was being

expelled. I felt that it was a very quick birth, very easy, very fast. I had a feeling that my mother was trying to rid herself of it. The placenta was out very quickly. After the birth I was aware of a hurried feeling in the room. No complications, yet. I did not feel like a newborn child. I felt relieved and just wanted to be cleaned up and put in the nursery. I was aware of other people's feelings in the delivery room, and I felt they were very mechanical and perfunctory, but had a feeling of relief that I was born. Incidentally, I have no knowledge at all of my actual birth experience, and have not been told about this." (Case A-399)

"In the birth canal, the contractions were pulses behind me. I feel long and slippery. After I'm born my feelings are that I'm tired and not too happy, and I'm still hesitant about this life. I'm very aware of too bright lights and cold, and I feel away from everyone." (Case A-396)

"When you asked about the birth canal, I saw that my spirit was looking over everything. I joined the body moments before the birth. My impression after birth was that the doctor's slap was *not* necessary. I felt indignant. I was aware that the doctor was badly hung over." (Case A-365)

"In the birth-canal experience I feel transparencies, and I see streaks of deep color. After I was born I felt very cold, like a breeze hitting you after you get out of a swimming pool. The doctors were very efficient and seemed amazed at my size. I consciously felt my breathing stop for a period of time, and my arms and legs tingled as though they were asleep, I also have a headache!" (Case A-359)

"The birth canal was an interesting trip. I was watching the bluish light at the end. The canal trip was an adventure, but the birth was rather mundane. After birth I felt calmer and I also experienced a stinging feeling on my skin. I heard someone in the delivery room say, 'Oh, what a fat boy!' " (Case A-342)

"When you asked about the birth canal, I felt I was stuck, because I wanted to stay inside. I didn't want to emerge. After I was born, all impressions were experienced totally. It was as though there was some ecstasy in a physical sensation alternating with stark fear. I was aware of the feelings of others in the delivery room." (Case A-340)

"I skipped the actual birth-canal experience but after birth I was aware of bright, awful lights. I was aware that my mother didn't want me and I was surprised and disappointed to discover it." (Case A-335)

"In the birth canal I felt heavy contractions, but they were smooth and silky. I came frontally, and I felt a large lump on my forehead. After birth I felt fear of the bright light and the noise. I was aware that my mother was ashamed of me because I was a homely baby." (Case A-334)

"In the birth canal I seemed to be straining and pressing on some kind of hard, muscular surface. It seems I can't wait to be born. As soon as I emerged I felt a great feeling of separation, and no more warmth and protection. The people in the delivery room were kind but efficient, and I felt distant from them." (Case A-314)

"The birth-canal experience for me was pleasant. I just moved down with smooth contractions. As soon as I was born I was aware of feeling very sensitive and vulnerable. I had a very high trust and awareness of others. I was aware that people around me were showing a mechanical attitude about the birth, but they touched me as tenderly as possible. Their standards were very gross compared to mine, but somehow I seemed to understand." (Case A-189)

"The birth canal seemed to me like a long tunnel, like I was diving. I felt afraid. As soon as I was born I was still very fearful, because I felt vulnerable and alone. Lots of impersonal people and flashing lights. My mother was asleep (anesthesia?) and no one held me or welcomed me, and I felt that familiar longing for love." (Case A-190)

"The birth-canal experience for me was of floating very easily in a blue-white liquid. I came through the canal easily, but when I got to the end I got frightened of the work I had to do, and I didn't want to come out. My impressions after birth were of bewilderment, fear, cold air, and I was shivering." (Case A-286)

"The birth canal for me was not unpleasant, it was like a quick rush. Right after birth I felt strong energy sensations, rather than saw pictures. It took me a while to see with my eyes, but I sensed energy. I felt the acceptance and awe of my mother, also her confusion as how to deal with me." (Case A-240)

"The birth-canal experience for me was painless, as if an innertube were passed over my head and down my shoulders and down past my feet—a squeezing sensation. When you asked my impressions after birth, I felt a tightening in my stomach, a sort of chill in the same area where I later developed pyloric stenosis at age thirteen. It seemed to me the doctors were unresponsive to my consciousness, and treated me as a nonentity, a mere thing or object." (Case A-239)

"In the birth canal I floated around with my feet first to keep from coming out. Then I got moved around to enable me to emerge head first. (The doctor used forceps.) After birth I felt nauseous and very resentful. The doctor didn't like doing the delivery, and I could feel it. My mother was relieved, though still shaky." (Case A-235)

"In the birth canal I found it hard to breathe and stuffy, and I was aware of pressure all over, especially on my head. I felt like I was flailing my arms. When I emerged I felt frightened and lonely, it seemed that there was too much space around me, I'm too open, I want my mother's warmth. My mother was happy, but the people in the delivery room were not overly efficient." (Case A-230)

"The birth-canal experience for me was most vivid. I could experience the warmth of the uterus and the muscular contractions forcing me down. I was experiencing moving downward, then this intense, agonizingly bright light, and my face contracting. I was vaguely aware of some thoughts the doctors and nurses had, and their feelings. It was not my present ego that accepted this idea, because I felt as an infant you're not supposed to be doing this. But I *was* telepathically aware of their feelings." (Case A-229)

"For me, the birth-canal experience was a pulsating one. My head came first and then shoulders and then all the way. I heard a man reassuring my mother that this one was going to live. The pulsating feeling is the same one I get quite often in meditation as energy flowing in currents through my body. It was surprising under hypnosis to discover this was my birth-canal experience." (Case A-223)

"For me, it seemed I was out of the birth canal quickly, as though I were pulled out. As soon as I emerged it was very scary with lots of lights. People were handling me in a very unloving way, very cold emotionally. I was aware of their feelings. They were doing their job and had good intentions. They were just not aware of their own insensibility and how much I could understand." (Case A-221)

"In the birth canal I felt the push, and I felt squished, and I was glad to be out of the canal and finally unfolding my wrinkled body. I felt my hands. They had been closed into my sides. My fingers at last could stretch. The doctor seemed to be giving me the most attention, holding me a minute while the nurse looked on. I had good feelings about him. I think my mom was out of it. I must comment that when you were giving suggestions, I felt somehow that I was outside of my real body." (Case A-155)

"I was unsure of what was coming in the birth-canal experience, but after birth I felt alienated and alone. I didn't want to be touched. I wanted to feel the warm water again. I was aware of other people's feelings in the delivery room, but I was distant from them and didn't want to be close to them. I was in a world of strangers and lost without Louis. (Louis is a twin who left the womb early because he had other things to do. But his spirit is helping me.)" (Case A-588)

"The birth-canal experience for me was smooth with no pain on my part, just a feeling of tightness. When I emerged I was cold, and I wanted my mother to hold and love me. It seemed like a long time from the birth experience to my mother's arms. It seemed like the people in the delivery room thought it was no big deal." (Case A-354)

"The birth-canal experience was fear of being closed in and wanting to be free. After I was born I felt great cold and difficulty in breathing. My spirit came in to stay at the time of birth. But I was aware of the feelings of others in the delivery room. They didn't think I'd live, and I wanted to tell them that I would." (Case A-361)

"The birth-canal experience for me was a feeling

that it was quite short, and I was very aware of darkness. When you asked the sensory impressions after birth, I seemed to be flashing in and out. There was a strong connection at the moment of your questions, as if I were awake then and had forgotten about it until now. I was just aware of light and noise and the feeling of losing something." (Case A-424)

"The birth-canal experience for me was uncomfortable. I was a breech birth and got pulled out with forceps. I found the physical sensations extremely unplesant. After I was born I felt bright lights and I was uncomfortable and had great pain. The doctor and nurse were worried and then relieved. I have to comment that why I was born was beyond me. I certainly didn't want to." (Case A-429)

"The birth-canal experience for me was tight and choking sensations. Immediately after birth I felt there was too much light. I knew the midwife felt everything went well. I was born at home, and after my ·birth I saw the bedroom with two windows, two chairs and a table at the end of the bed, a basket on top of the table and big, fluffy feather beds." (Case A-193)

"I came into my body as I came out of my mother. I felt blinding light and I felt helpless. I was being moved around by giants. I felt very cold. The people in the room seemed hurried and uncaring." (Case A-147)

"When you asked about the birth, I had actual physical sensations in the here and now. My body jerked and I was extremely cold and started to shake. My impressions after birth were, 'Well, here I am!'" (Case A-64)

"It seemed to take every ounce of effort I had in the birth-canal experience to get born. It was very slimy with a lot of mucous around. Immediately after birth I felt intense cold and my mouth and throat were clogged. It seemed like I was getting a huge input of sensory stuff. I was aware that the doctor was very matter-of-fact." (Case A-149)

"The birth-canal experience for me was very uncomfortable and tight, and I had a feeling of being shoved. After I was born, my eyes were hurting, and I was cold and felt very helpless. There was excitement in the room and people were almost festive. I saw great orange translucent cords inside the fetus. They were glassy-like bulbous nodes, and I felt myself shifting through these obstacles in order to be born. They were very flexible, and they hugged me as I emerged." (Case A-152)

"I went through the birth-canal experience okay, but after I was born I couldn't breathe. I have felt constriction around my throat all my life in connection with this experience. I almost died at birth. The cause was unclear, whether it was caused by morphine medication or a cord around my neck or something else. I was aware that other people were worried and scared about the condition of the baby." (Case A-124)

"In the birth-canal experience I had a visual image of leaving the uterus through the canal and my body twitched when I came out. (My body here in this room.) I felt after birth that somehow I was standing in the air, facing my mother, but I wasn't really seeing her. I had a lot of joy at the sensory experiences, and then I had a lot of anger. I don't know what the anger was from." (Case A-108)

"As I was entering the world I could feel the warmth of the part of me inside and cold on my head and shoulders moving down my body as I pulled out. I felt cold, and quite fragile, and I also had a feeling of excitement after I was born. I was aware of relief on the part of the people involved in the birth, like they'd overcome some problem. My feelings were that I knew it would be all right." (Case A-266)

"In the birth-canal experience, all I can say is, 'Why couldn't I have been born inside a flower bud in a beautiful flower garden?' My impressions after birth were that I was in the wrong place. Everyone wanted a boy, and I was the fifth girl." (Case A-42)

"The birth-canal experience for me was very smooth and quick. After birth, I felt brightness, and after a few seconds a large shudder or sigh. The people in the delivery room were very busy and brusque, and I felt alone. Most of this trip was vague, except for the very real physical feeling a few seconds after birth— like a big, soft electric jolt." (Case A-94)

"When you asked about the birth-canal experience I didn't feel anything because I felt like I was in and out of my body. Then I emerged and I was choking. I felt fingers in my throat as I was being held upside down. I had no feeling for my mother's awareness, except perhaps relief, and I knew there was a clinical attitude from the two doctors in the hospital." (Case B-101)

"I didn't get much from the birth-canal experience, but after you asked the sensory impressions after birth, the words came to me, 'Well, you can't go back now!' I was aware that one nurse there scratched my face at birth, and I was scared. My body actually jumped at this impression of the scratched face." (Case A-553)

"When you asked about the birth-canal experience, my heartbeat quickened, and gradually I felt rhythmic moving back and forth, down the birth canal. Not unpleasant, but it could have been overwhelming had I experienced it for a longer period of time. After I emerged the light hurt my eyes, and my eyes watered. I was dimly aware of others' feeling in the delivery room. I felt that the men in the room were being unsupportive. I felt superfluous somehow." (Case A-519)

"The birth-canal experience for me was hazy, but I was aware that my shoulder was caught and my neck twisted. After birth I was in great pain in my neck and shoulder. I was afraid of falling and the nurse was bouncing me up and down, and I was screaming. My father and the nurse were laughing at me as I screamed." (Case A-418)

"The experience in the birth canal was harsh and dark. But when I finally was born I felt relief. I felt sore and unhappy after birth, but when cleaned and dried I felt content at last. I was aware that my parents were a little put out, and made large plans for the future, and so they tried to make up for their reluctance to become parents, but I knew the truth." (Case A-557)

"The birth-canal experience was uncomfortable. I thought I was dying. After I emerged the light was very strong, and I felt very cold. I had a feeling of being lifted in space—I felt scared with nothing to hold onto, out of balance—I felt teary at being so helpless again, even though I had all the intelligence of an adult." (Case A-23)

"When you asked about the birth-canal experience, I felt pressure and waves of movement. I thought I didn't particularly want to be bothered with this mess. After birth I immediately felt cold, and then I had a feeling of oops! They find out I'm not a boy. One nurse was impressionable. (She must be new.) The others were cold, and this was old-hat for them. I have the knowledge that I must play the game. My mother was glad it was over, but my father was deeply disappointed about the sex." (Case A-201)

"My birth-canal experience was easy, and it was slick. That is contrary to what I've been told. This was a very vivid feeling. After birth, I was in a white room. I was held and stroked and fondled and warmed. I was aware the others were glad I was a girl, but it was not a whole-hearted welcome. I think there was a general worry about something." (Case A-165)

"It was as though I took a final trip inside the fetus, down the birth canal, and it was like a door shut and locked. As soon as I was born, I felt like I was going into a new class, I had a ready-to-learn feeling." (Case A-185)

"When you asked about the birth-canal experience, I had an expectancy of trauma, but my sensory impressions after birth were of settling in, with feelings of good, high-spirited looking forward now to this life and what it will offer, as well as friends whom I will meet. I was aware of an emotionally charged state in the hospital room, with the chaotic emotions of those present. Like in the birth canal, I felt distant from it all." (Case A-204)

"When you asked about the birth-canal experience, I felt pressure on my head, and no feeling in my legs. After birth, I felt my legs were numb and my lungs raw. It seemed to be just business to the people in the delivery room. My legs felt like they were asleep here in this room, but when I got up after the hypnosis I found they weren't. A very odd feeling. I guess I really was hypnotized." (Case A-285)

"The birth-canal experience went very fast for me. As soon as I emerged my first thought was, 'Did I make the right choice?' I felt cool air, sounds, light." (Case A-481)

"As the birth process begins I get dizzy, and my world goes round. I feel, 'Okay, let's get out of here.' I feel bright lights and cold. I'm annoyed with the nurse who is patting my shoulder. My mother is out of it, and the doctor and nurses are happy that I'm a very healthy baby." (Case A-418)

"The birth canal for me was dark and cramped, and I didn't want to go just yet. I had been very comfortable. After birth I felt cold and light. People were making too much noise and it hurt my ears, and the light hurt my eyes. I was aware that the doctor wanted to go home and everyone was tired. Strange—I wanted to be born until I had to go, then I didn't want to." (Case A-141)

"In the birth canal I was aware that I was not ready to leave. The body was turned and forceps were used. After birth I still felt reluctance, and I was not ready. I felt anxiety, but I was excited. I did feel my mother's joy and her touch. I was not aware of anyone else." (Case A-325)

"In the birth canal I felt pressure on my head, I was struggling. I tried to help with my arms, but found I had to do all the work with my head. After birth I felt confused and I seemed to be frowning hard. I felt free movement of my head and arms, but I was uncomfortable with the light." (Case A-349)

"In the birth canal I felt a pulsating feeling and I had real cramps in my stomach. Mucous came into my head (this is under hypnosis). After birth, I was aware of the sharp lights, and loud sounds. The people in the delivery room seemed very businesslike." (Case A-92)

"I slid through the birth canal easily with a little squirming, and afterwards I wanted to be cleaned up. I was aware that the doctor was preoccupied or resentful about something, and my mother was anxious to see that I was okay." (Case A-395)

"I felt angry in the birth canal because I was being hurried ahead of the time I wanted to go. As soon as

I was born I was aware of a bright white wall, only about a yard in front of me. I wasn't aware of other people's feelings, because I was so conscious of my intense anger." (Case A-306)

"The birth-canal experience for me was very vague. I had the sensation of my hands being over my head as I left the canal. After birth things were most unpleasant. I seemed to cry a lot." (Case A-290)

"When you asked about the birth canal, I remember my head being out and the rest of my body still in my mother. I was looking up at the ceiling. After birth I was aware of green hospital gowns and bright lights. I was aware of other people's feelings, and I had the understanding of an adult, not a child. I just listened and observed." (Case B-105)

"The birth-canal experience for me was like going through a tunnel, then blue clarity, then yellow, then pure light. After birth I had a good feeling. I liked the water I was washed in and the warmth of being wrapped up. I was aware of the feelings of others in the room, and that my family was delighted that I was a beautiful baby girl." (Case B-1)

"The birth-canal experience for me was wet and warm. After I was born I felt cold and other sensations. Touch especially—others who were touching me felt cold. I was aware that others in the room were just busy, so much activity compared to the womb. The feelings of being born seemed very real. It appeared that I was an observer to the first forming of the fetus, but also felt I was experiencing what the fetus was." (Case B-3)

"The feeling in the birth canal was rushing, warm, painful. After birth I felt very cold and frightened, and unwanted. I was aware of the feelings of the others in the room, and my mother feels rejection.

My father has mixed feelings. An older aunt was assistant to the doctor, and since I was not breathing, she literally made me breathe." (Case B-34)

"The birth-canal experience for me felt tight and slightly wet. I was afraid after I was born the doctor or whoever held me would drop me. I was aware of other people's feelings, and everyone was quiet and concerned." (Case B-38)

"The birth-canal experience for me was one of spinning and sinking. After birth I saw a white room with brown wooden furniture. (A hospital delivery room fifty years ago?) I wasn't aware of other people's feelings. This was a strange experience." (Case B-42)

"I didn't have any pain during the birth-canal experience. After birth the lights were harsh, but I was happy to be born. My mother was very happy, and everyone in the room was joking and happy, and I seemed to be laughing inside." (Case B-96)

"In the birth canal, some force kept pushing me. I couldn't do anything about it, because there was nothing to brace myself with or hang on to. Immediately after birth I felt a sudden rush of cold air, bright lights, people wearing funny clothes. My mother seemed relieved that labor was over. She fell asleep. People's attitudes seemed to be concern that I came out all right." (Case A-20)

"In the birth canal, I felt like I burst out into excruciating noise. It hurt my ears very much. I couldn't get my breath, and it was very hard for me to breathe for a while. I was aware of others' emotions all around me." (Case A-75)

"It seemed as though I just swam out of the birth canal. As I swam out I became human. Immediately after birth I felt that they were pulling me unnecessarily. I felt drained and angry. I felt raw from the light, the air, everything. They were so *rough*. The atmosphere was rude. I had expected playing, but it was all commotion, and I longed to be back in space where everything was light." (Case A-339. This subject had an urgent desire to get "down there" to play, and felt that someone was trying to keep her from getting born.)

"The birth-canal experience was one of 'Ah—here I go! Exciting!' Immediately after birth I felt light, cold, and pain when I try to breathe. I hurt and I'm shocked and I'm angry, because it's not all fun and games. A woman takes me roughly. She's angry, and she doesn't like me. I've offended her somehow. My mother is too tired and hurt to care much about me, and she leaves. This was a real bummer. I had actual tears on this trip. I really wanted to go back to that outer-space light." (Case A-374. This subject also chose eagerly to be born, and was anxious to get started.)

"The birth experience for me was swimming quickly on my back, moving my arms rapidly to get out fast. As soon as I was born, I felt anger, and I was aware that I had clenched fists. I was lying on my back screaming, and my feet were also clenched. I was in a delivery room, and the hospital personnel are running around and there is great commotion. My mother is asleep, but I have no response from her. After a short time my anger leaves, and I feel very happy and energetic." (Case A-375)

"The birth-canal experience for me was a definite struggle and some hesitancy. Immediately after birth I thought, 'I want to go back home!' The delivery-room people seemed to be making plans for the evening—dinner, dates, etc. I was aware that my dad was very pleased and happy." (Case A-140)

"To me, the birth-canal experience was unpleasant. I was being forced out against my will. I was angry and afraid, and I felt helpless. After birth the lights were too bright and no one was there to greet me. Everyone was very professional going around congratulating each other, but that didn't make me feel any better. I wanted to be reassured that it would be all right." (Case A-401)

"I was aware that my mother was very fearful, so I came early through the birth canal so she would not worry, and to make it easier for her. After birth I remember thinking that people are silly because they didn't seem to know what babies want. The doc didn't make it until after it was over, and he was uptight. The intern was happy. The nurses liked their job and thought I was beautiful." (Case A-422)

"In the birth canal I can see and feel the canal as warm, strong, supportive, helping me to move out, even though firm, and I had to do the moving. After birth I felt bright lights and cold. I liked the process of being born, but I didn't like it when I came out into the world. It was noisy, bright and cold, and then only later did I feel warm again. I was aware of others' feelings, and I felt a feeling of cold, and I was disappointed that the joy I felt about being born wasn't met on the outside. I seemed to be clear and aware, but the other people didn't know that." (Case A-345)

"The birth-canal experience for me was tight and constricted, especially my feet. After I was born I felt vertigo from being lifted and moved too quickly. I was aware of unpleasant bright lights and rough handling, my dense body was unpleasant, and I had mucus in my eyes and ears and mouth. I was aware of other people's feelings. My mother was spaced out, and the nurses were busy and indifferent." (Case A-493)

"It was sort of gooey and yucky inside the birth

canal, although warm. I fought to get out. I was terrified and I wanted to go back to prebirth (wherever I was before). I felt alone and scared. When I was born I felt cold and was aware of lots of light and noise. I was only aware of other people's feelings just a little bit. I seemed to be more concerned with how uncomfortable I was, and I started screaming." (Case A-231)

"The feeling in the birth canal was that it was pretty tight, and I felt, 'Kick, kick—get it over with.' I cried when I got out, because I wanted to stay close to the body—my mother's body—that I came from. I wanted to grab her and hold on. I was aware that the doctor was happily pleased, that I was a great joy to him. I got no reaction from my mother because she seemed to be asleep. I felt that being born into this present life was a stupid nuisance. I wanted to emerge in this life fast and it was too long for me to go through the fetus and birth process." (Case A-211)

"I didn't want to experience the birth so I didn't go through this and didn't enter until after birth. Then I saw the bedroom and the doctor and the people in the room (I was born at home). I didn't like the idea of being squeezed into this little body, but sort of said to myself, 'Well, here goes!' and plunged in, like jumping into cold water. The people in the room seemed to be happy and pleased." (Case A-234)

"In the birth canal I seemed to be coming through head down and turned over, and then I became head up. I think someone turned me rather than my turning myself. After birth I didn't know where I was and I couldn't open my eyes. I couldn't get out of my body to see what the room looked like and who else was there. I laid still for a long time, and I felt resigned to it all. (Case A-191. This subject was born in spite of advice not to come to this family.)

"The birth-canal experience for me was slow torture. I had a feeling of being crushed—there was not enough room—pain, and pressure. After I was born I felt the cold and that there was too much light. There was pain especially in my head and face. I was aware of other people's feelings. My mother had a feeling of relief from pain, but also some disgust. There was indifference on the part of all the hospital attendants, except for one warm-hearted nurse." (Case A-143)

"In the birth canal I felt constricted and it was terrifying. There was a compression fracture coming out. I was aware of being held by my grandfather, who delivered me, after I was born. My mother was out of it. I was lonely and bewildered, as they only pretended to rejoice, having wanted a boy." (Case A-156)

"When you asked about the birth-canal experience, I wasn't really identified with the baby. The birth was somewhat difficult and I watched it respond. After I was born, I looked at it first, because I still had some clear consciousness. It was like my mind was too big for this little body. I was aware that people in the delivery room worked with dispatch and purpose." (Case A-443)

"In the birth canal I am squeezing through, but it's not unpleasant. After I get born, I am struck by light and cold on my wet skin. I am upside down and helpless, and not helped emotionally at all. I squeeze my eyes tight and bear it as best I can. The doctor seemed busy about the business of birth and unconcerned with me as a person. My mother is out under anesthesia." (Case A-194)

"The birth canal just seemed warm but tight to me. After birth I am aware of someone trying to open and examine my eyes. I have heat sensations. I was aware that other people were running around frantically, because possibly I would die. I was trying to close off and disappear. I was premature and got the impression (in this hypnotic trip) this was an effort on my part and my mother's because she didn't want me, and I really didn't want to be born. (Case A-261)

"The birth-canal experience for me was strong. It was quite startling and not bad at all. I sent my mom messages to just feel it as sensations and not pain. She was drugged, but that didn't matter. After birth I was aware of loud noises and bright lights and it was irritating. I felt my baby's body was so amazingly strong and powerful. I was aware of my own jerky movements. I was clearly aware of other people's attitudes. The nurses went about their business and the doc, too, but he and they were pleased, and Mom was pleased, but pooped. I was very happy to be coming into this life. I especially loved my mom because she seemed just super to me. I worried I might be very sad, but I thought it would just have to be okay, anyway, after I was born." (Case A-327)

"When you asked about the birth canal, my chest hurt, as it started and then stopped, and then intensified. On the outside there was a lot of activity, and I saw white, blurry figures very active and busy. My upper chest in the bronchial area hurt very badly. (I was a serious problem at birth, and baptized twice because of doctor's fear of losing me. It was a problem through childhood [asthma] which now has settled into very occasional hay fever.)" (Case A-471)

"I felt the birth-canal experience to be suffocating. I felt the canal pressing in on me, and I saw some colors like pale yellow, and some purplish dull-red. I blocked the experiences after birth, because I know I had a black eye at birth, and I was afraid I would fantasize it rather than experience it. I did feel discomfort and pain in my back and between my shoulder blades. (I was mishandled at birth.) When you asked if I were aware of other people's feelings, for some reason I felt like laughing at them, I'm not sure why. I think it was because they had no idea who I really was and what birth was all about. It's interesting because I expect them to be blasé because this was a hospital. Instead they were silly, sentimental, happy, and this somehow seemed even funnier to me." (Case A-520)

"In the birth canal I was still just next to the body, but then I was in it and then out of it and could observe. After I was born I felt wet and I know I had a bloody forehead that was bruised. I was slow to realize that my head hurt. I was aware that someone in the room said I looked funny. That somehow bothered me and would stay with me, even though I also heard them say I would be okay later." (Case A-482)

"The birth-canal experience for me wasn't smooth, but in jerks, surrounded by softness. It was almost unyielding though. I remember the tremendous bursting desire to breathe and feel my limbs free, to *stretch*. After I was born, the first breath seemed burning and almost painful, and I was coughing and choking. Before being washed, my skin was burning and painfully being tightened by drying ambiotic fluid and itching. Unfortunately, I was scrubbed by some idiot with a horrible scratchy sponge. It was a very cold delivery room. Everyone was quite aware of my mother's feelings about the birth. I kept hearing her say, 'I don't want it, I don't want it.'" (Case A-348)

"The birth-canal experience for me was very strange. At the start of it, I came out of the trance state with an unpleasant, shock-like start, and opened my eyes. After birth, as I went back into trance, I was aware of a feeling in my own body of being a baby.

My arms especially seemed to wave about and lack muscular control. My impression was that my mother was asleep." (Case A-206)

"In the birth experience I felt some hand grabbing me out by my feet, and I seemed to be clinging to my mother's insides. After birth I was aware of the fetal remains and blood dripping from my eyes. There was also a bright light, and I was being hassled by all the operating-room people. I sensed that they were wrapping me up in the wrong things, deceitful and inhibiting things. I felt very negative about the whole experience of being born." (Case A-324)

"As you asked about the birth canal, I was aware of pressure on my forehead, and I became aware of a pulsing, tightening feeling on my head. After birth, I wanted very much to be held and enclosed. I was aware of some impatience at my mother's uncertainty, but I know her joy of me was strong." (Case A-341)

"When you asked about the birth canal, I felt very angry. I wanted to get out and my mother doesn't want me to get out. I'm kicking, fighting, screaming. After birth I have relief, but I'm still upset. My thought was, 'So that's the place I wanted to get into so much!' I was aware of other people's feelings after my birth. My grandmother was very nasty. I first thought it was a snotty nurse, and then I realized it was my grandmother." (Case A-352)

"When you asked about the birth canal, I had a strong physical feeling of push, push, push. After birth, I didn't have too much impression. Everybody was very quiet. I did feel intense cold, and I felt very alone. My mother was happy, but for some reason I felt she wasn't ready for me." (Case A-494)

"To me the birth canal was like going down a dark tunnel toward life, and being tightly fitted against that tunnel. After birth, I was aware of very harsh light that hurts my eyes and a lot of noise. I hear swirling, echoing sounds. I was aware that my mother was disappointed because I was the wrong sex." (Case A-360)

"When you asked about the birth-canal experience, I felt my heart accelerating. It was like rushing down a slide. After I was born, it was a sterile-looking room and very quiet. It felt weird being in a little body. The people in the room were kind, but they seemed indifferent to me." (Case A-7)

"In the birth canal I felt pressure and pain on my head, especially the right side of my head. There was pressure on my sternum, and there was difficulty in breathing. After birth I felt the harshness of light, cold and the limitation of the body. I knew I didn't want to be here." (Case A-144)

"I wasn't aware of much in the birth canal, but after I was born, I felt confusion and bewilderment. I thought, 'What do I do now?' There was no contact from the surroundings because of my premature birth, and I am treated apart, special. I cannot join my mother and start life right away." (Case A-420)

"In the birth canal, I saw a mucousy-red surrounding. My large head almost burst out. Everyone was worried about my mother because I was so big. I was very much alive and active. But after birth I felt very sorry and unhappy. I was aware that other people in the delivery room thought I was beautiful, but I knew my mother didn't really want me, because of the responsibility involved. I really didn't realize the sadness and unhappiness involved in my birth until this experience." (Case A-238)

"In the birth canal I felt suffocation. I was aware in my here-and-now of breathing and trying to make a suffocation feeling stop. After birth I was very, very cold. I was aware of other people's feelings after I was born in the delivery room. Every person that touches me emanates a definite attitude." (Case A-98)

"The birth-canal experience for me was one of moving very rapidly down, much excitement, and a final burst-through. After birth I feel there are other scattered energies and intensities around me. I was aware of other people's feelings in a very clear perceptive sort of way. Things were very obvious, but not specific or explainable in an intellectual sense." (Case A-101)

"When you asked about the birth canal, I felt my head pounding, and I had a feeling I was about to burst. I had a headache. After birth I felt uncomfortable, and it felt strange because I was so tiny for who I really was inside! I felt like I was busy analyzing my mother, grandfather, and father. I was aware of great joy from my mother and grandmother and pride." (Case A-351)

"I came down toward the old house when you asked about being in the birth canal. I almost changed my mind, but I knew I had to be born for a reason. Right after birth I was aware of my mother and father crying. My grandmother, grandfather, aunt and uncle were there. The atmosphere was emotionally charged with ambiguous feelings, and the strongest feeling I had was fear, and a deep feeling of loneliness." (Case A-489)

"I felt like I had to join the fetus, because it wouldn't have survived if I hadn't joined consciousness with it earlier than I had planned. After I was born I felt heavy and there was a denseness, like it was much, much heavier than I could have imagined. It was very hard." (Case A-393)

"For me, the birth experience was pushing my face across flesh to the end of the tunnel. There was light at the end of the tunnel. My mom was unconscious, but I see yellow walls and bright lights. There are cold people who whisk me out of the room. Everything went too fast." (Case A-313)

"The birth-canal experience for me was fearful. During the recall my body was trembling and tingling all over. Also it seemed to be twisting in opposite directions slightly. I was crying immediately upon entering the outside environment. I was aware that everyone around me thought my birth was very routine." (Case A-330)

"In the birth canal I experienced reluctance and it was very difficult to be born. After my birth I felt a strong sensation of pain. The lights were too strong. My whole body is screaming with pain. My mother has abandoned me, she's not there (out under anesthesia), My mother has left, and other people in the room were very efficient but without much heart. Not a very pleasant entry into the world." (Case A-284)

I won't summarize these many stories about getting born. Though it is clear to me that most of my subjects, no matter how enthusiastically they chose to enter the world, found the actual experience one of loneliness and alienation from the "land of light" that they lost when they once more entered the physical world.

VIII

ADOPTED CHILDREN, PREMATURE BIRTHS, CAESAREANS

The great majority of my subjects were single births, born at term. But, as in any group of 750 people, there were cases that didn't follow the usual pattern.

One of the most interesting of these peculiarities is the phenomenon of twins. Twins occur with relative rarity in the human species, and when they do they are of two types. They may be two eggs fertilized during the same cycle by the same father, but containing a different combination of genes from both mother and father. These we call fraternal twins. The other phenomenon, more rare in the human species, is that of the single egg that divides and becomes two separate embryos. These embryos contain precisely the same genetic material, unlike the separate eggs of fraternal twins. In a profound sense, the phenomenon of identical twins is a form of cloning. The cloning occurs after the first cell division, resulting in the development of two absolutely identical embryos which develop into two identical but quite separate bodies.

The phenomenon of identical twins has long fascinated humanity. Twins are difficult to tell apart by the casual observer, though the mother and intimates of identical twins are able to distinguish them. How is it that identical twins can be different in any way? If they have the same genetic material, what is it that alters their bodies enough to make distinctions between the two possible? One reason you can tell identical twins apart is that they are mirror images of each other. A whorl of hair on the left side of the head on one twin will be a whorl of hair on the right side of the other twin. But apart from these discriminations based on the bilateral symmetry effect, anyone who knows a pair of identical twins will immediately see the differences. One may have a slightly more fleshy nose, another set of twins may display quite different facial expressions. It is perhaps in the eyes of identical twins that one can most clearly tell them apart. It is as though in essence a personality comes through so that one can clearly tell whether you are dealing with twin A or with twin B.

As identical twins grow apart in age, and each begins life development on their own upon emerging from childhood, these distinctions become more marked. Twins may vary in weight, facial features, and in many other characteristics as well, once they begin to experience life apart from a similar environment. Yet it is still very easy to see that they are of the same genetic material.

Tests on twins have revealed many similarities in the choices, intellectual abilities, susceptibility to disease, and even age at time of death. We often marvel at the similarities, but seem incurious as to the differences that can occur in identical twins, both in life experiences and in appearance in later life.

One of the theories of reincarnation is that the DNA molecules, the carrier of the hereditary material or "blueprint" for the body and mind, are the explanation for the fact that people can "recall" past lives. Briefly, this theory states that a memory of all the previous experiences of our species and even of our evolutionary development from one-cell organisms to mammals, is coded in the DNA molecules within each cell of our body. According to this theory, we are able to get in touch with past experiences of animals and other people through using the DNA molecule as a mode of transmitting experiences. This idea has a lot of attraction for those of us in our society who clearly feel that some physical mechanism must be present to explain any mental event. It somehow seems more scientific than the notion that the soul or spirit lives through different experiences in different bodies and is able to recall this.

If the DNA theory is true, identical twins would remember the same past lives! This would be an interesting theory to test. I did have eleven twins in my sample group of 750 subjects. However, only one had the identical twin present at the regression.

This pair of identical twins had quite different past lives, though each chose separate time periods to explore. During the birth experience they felt they were in telepathic communication with each other. One twin freely chose to be born, while the other was reluctant to experience physical life again. Both reported that they had known their twin in past lives. No details of the relationship in past lives were reported.

It would be an exciting research project to find ten

sets of identical twins and regress them individually, both to past lives and to the birth experience. The ideal would be to regress twins separately at different times, making sure that they had not communicated in the interim. Then it would be possible to find out if they had recorded precisely the same past lives, and precisely the same birth experience. If they did, it would go far toward supporting the DNA or hereditary concept of past-life recall memories. Though I didn't have these ideal conditions, I was still able to get impressions from twins as to their relationships to their twin prior to birth, and even in past lives.

The results were remarkably consistent. My subjects who were twins reported that they had known their twin intimately in past lives, and were with them in the period between lives. Their relationship was extremely close, not apparently because they were twins, but they decided to come into life as twins because they were close!

"My twin wanted to come into life at this time and talked me into going along with her. She seemed to have more karma to work out than I did, or at least was more eager to go. I agreed to come with her and we chose twin fetuses. I was not in the fetus until just before birth, nor was my twin. Then I had the impression that we were arguing about which twin fetus we would choose—which one would be the brown-haired baby, and which the blonde. Then we were in the fetus and she was in a hurry to get born. I hung back and was reluctant to enter the world. I became aware that she was urging me to come along and to hurry up."

This subject had a very interesting real-life experience. While she was going through this emotional experience on the birth trip, the telephone rang. The workshop was being held in her home. Someone who was not hypnotized answered the phone, and it wasn't until I awoke the subjects from hypnosis that we heard what the phone call was. It was my subject's twin sister, calling from 2,000 miles away. She had had a sudden telepathic flash that her sister was in some kind of difficulty or experiencing emotions, and had phoned to see if she were all right.

Apparently, my subject's reluctance to be born was conveyed to her twin sister many miles distant. Other subjects who were twins reported similar experiences. They had known their twin before in a past life as a sister or brother; one had known her twin as a lover, another had known her twin as a teacher in a past life. They were aware before they were born that they would be living together as twins, and all looked forward to the experience.

One subject who was a twin had an interesting experience.

"When you took me to the time before I was born, I was aware that I was there with someone I thought of as Louis. We were very close, and he was urging me to be born. I was aware that it was necessary for me to go through another lifetime, that I had learned enough in the between-life stage, and that I had to go back to earth again. Louis was advising me and assuring me that he would watch over me. We chose twin fetuses. I wasn't in the fetus until just before birth. I became aware with a growing feeling of unhappiness that Louis was withdrawing from the fetus that was his. Apparently he would not be born with me, or would not live with me as a twin. I became aware that he was saying reluctantly that he could not come with me, but that he would be in my dream states and in touch with me in other ways to help sustain me through what would be a difficult lifetime.

Louis was a stillborn fetus, but I lived. I am aware of a figure in my dreams who is counseling me and reassuring me. I guess it's Louis!"

Other subjects reported that people they knew in this life had been twins of theirs in a past life. Again, this was not common, as twins are not common. One subject wrote, in response to the question about karmic ties, "When you asked if I knew my father to be, I suddenly realized that he had been a twin of mine in a past life. We had been close at that time, and I looked forward to knowing him again. But this time we would be as father-child rather than as twin sisters."

Another subject saw a friend in this life as someone who had been a twin of hers in a past life. "We've always felt unusually close. Sometimes we have telepathic experiences with each other. I wonder if this is because we were twins in a past life?"

The interesting thing about the data I have on twins is its relationship to the idea of cloning. A clone is essentially a reproduction of an individual by controlling the genetic environment. An embryo is created bearing precisely the same genetic material as one parent (either a man or a woman). The fetus developed with just the genetic material of one parent is carried in the womb through implantation, and goes through the normal stages, emerging at birth. The idea behind the excitement generated by cloning is that in producing separate physical individuals, we will presumably be recreating the same personality. In this way we can all achieve immortality by creating new bodies for ourselves. This idea, while very attractive to people who don't believe that consciousness is in any way separate from the physical brain, poses a number of difficulties.

The closest we can come to analyzing what will

happen to the mind and spirit of a clone is to examine what happens with identical twins. If we are all blank tablets, minds waiting to be developed through the experiences of the physical stimuli around us, then presumably what differences are observed in identical twins are a result of small environmental differences. Mother may treat one twin slightly different from another. An extreme example of this would be a phenomenon like triplets and even quintuplets. These are examples of clones occurring naturally.

I believe it has been established beyond reasonable doubt that the personalities of identical twins and indeed of quadruplets and quintuplets are different, even though the genetic material is the same. One quintuplet may show a great deal of physical activity from birth on, while his fellow quintuplet may be passive. These differences are seen from the earliest stage of infancy, and increase as the twins, triplets and quadruplets grow up. Each one seems to select from the environment around them specific stimuli that appeal to them, and each develops in his own way. They are different spirits. If anyone among my readers knows of twins, triplets, or quadruplets who display the same personality characteristics and interests, I would appreciate hearing from them.

According to the evidence of the birth trip under hypnosis reported in this book, these souls or spirits may have chosen to come together in identical bodies, but their reasons for being born, their motivations, feelings, and karmic relationships are different. This is why they do seem to be unique individuals in spite of the identical genetic material.

What would happen if we were able to clone ourselves, by reproducing our own genetic material? Wouldn't the results be the same as those we see with multiple births? An individual created out of our own cellular structure would likely be even more different than identical twins prove to be. We went through infancy, childhood and adolescence in a different period of history than would be experienced by our clone. All of the environmental influences that did help to shape our lives would be quite different for our clone. So while there might be a resemblance in the experiences of our clone to our own experiences, the likelihood is that the resemblance would be slight. This is true if one holds to the environmental notion of the development of the personality.

If the evidence of my subjects under hypnosis on the birth trip is valid, all that would happen if we used cloning rather than the usual method of creating embryos would be that more souls could enter the earth to experience physical life because more vehicles would be available to them. This has already happened in our historical time period, as the infant mortality rate has decreased significantly and the birth rate has increased in relationship to the death rate. This has made it possible for more souls to experience physical existence, and to experience full lifetimes rather than having been cut off in childhood through epidemic disease or poor nutrition. It's hard to see what difference cloning would make, except perhaps to limit the gene pool.

The research scientists in the laboratories who are working with cloning explain that they are merely trying to find ways to improve animal protein. Geneticists have been messing around with cows for many years, trying to produce the perfect beast for a minimum amount of money. We've been playing God with other mammals for a very long time, with no compunction. It can be said at this point that after many years of miraculously redoing cows into our idea of a juicy steak, we are now faced with the problem that we've been developing breeds of meat animals that give us a lot more protein than we need. The poor cow, having devoted its life to livestock breeders in the interests of feeding man, now stands suspect of providing us with more cholesterol and unneeded nutrients that are adding to the dangers of our comfortable lifestyle. I myself have always had a special fondness for the cow, with its capacity to produce butter, ice cream and hamburgers, all of which I delight in. I figure that human beings are at the top of the food chain, and the cows should keep busy munching their salad greens and turning it into beefsteak for me to enjoy in a short period of time. It takes months of salad eating for the cow to produce enough calories so that I can consume it in one brief sitting and sail cheerfully on, nourished by the energy provided by the salad going through the cow. So I have a lot to thank the geneticists for.

Now that I am middle-aged, and helplessly addicted to cholesterol-producing agents, I find that nature was right all along. As I no longer wander the fields collecting my own salad (I let the cow do that), I now find that I have to go in for jogging and physical fitness exercises to make up for the deficit. Even the best of our cows no longer jog much; they're fed special vitamins and food supplements and allowed to lie around so they develop lots of nice marbled fat for our beefsteaks. Unfortunately, our original genetic material was designed to last us fourscore and ten, eating the food crop around us and expending a lot of energy in collecting them. The whole thing seems to have come full circle. We now have movie stars paid in the millions daintily munching away on sparse salad while spending several hours a day "getting in shape" by exercising. It seems to me it was probably more fun to go roaming around hunting our food, getting our healthy exercise; at the same time getting our food fresh.

This long digression aside, it seems that cloning is a development of our society and an attempt to control the evolutionary process in the animals we raise for food. If we could produce one perfect beefsteak on the hoof and clone that animal, we'd all be able to eat the same beefsteak. Cloning seems unlikely even in this limited application, as now we are told that we shouldn't eat beef, but rather chicken and fish. Fish seem to clone themselves rather successfully; at least no one as far as I know is working on the development of the perfect trout. Trouts are left to work on that project.

So while cloning seems like an exciting new development in mankind, because again it implies this God-like ability to totally alter our environment, including the environment of our own body, to me it holds relatively little interest. We are all supposed to be getting back to the animals we originally were anyway, so the "new improved version" will still have to eat alfalfa sprouts and jog once a day. Why not stick with the same old animal? The same old human body that has served down through the millennia?

Six of my 750 subjects reported that they were premature, born at six to seven months of fetal development. Interestingly, all of these subjects felt that they were not in the fetus until just before birth. Three of the subjects reported that they were counseled by "others" all during the time of fetal development, and were told that they needed to hurry into the body because birth was occurring before expected. Two of these subjects reported life in the incubator or life-support system where they were placed immediately after their premature births. These subjects said that they were not in their body during much of this time, floating in and out as so many subjects had reported doing. One subject reported that the life-sustaining machine was pleasant for her because it enabled her to breathe. She was aware immediately after birth of extreme difficulty in breathing. But this subject didn't stay around the incubator much either.

One subject who came at six months' fetal development gave an interesting reason for this. She reported that she felt unwanted by her mother, and also said she was not eager to be born. "It was as though there was a collaboration between the two of us; we wanted to separate and not spend so much time in the fetal development stage."

Another fourteen of my subjects wrote on their data sheets that they had been born by Caesarean section. This was a low percentage, but this is because most of my subjects were age thirty or older. Caesarean section was relatively rare in the past, though in the past few years it has become increasingly common. Were the experiences of being born by Caesarean section different from the experiences of more normal birth-canal expulsion?

Apparently, there were some difficulties experienced by the subjects who had Caesarean births. One subject seemed to be glad because he reported that he had been struggling to be born, "My head was pushing against some immovable obstacle and I felt increasingly frantic." This subject went on to explain, "Then suddenly I was lifted up and drawn out into the world. Apparently, they had had to do a Caesarean because the labor had gone on too long, and I could not be born the normal way. I felt resentment at being suddenly jerked up, but I felt glad to be able to take a breath. I seemed to know that I would now live."

Another subject born by Caesarean section reported,

"I am not really ready to be born. I have joined the fetus, and am just getting ready to start when suddenly I am jerked up out into the air. I am held rather casually up above my mother, and I experience severe anxiety. I am afraid of falling, and I am assaulted by feelings of cold and bright light. The greatest fear is that somehow I will fall." This subject went on to report under "Additional Comments" at the bottom of the page, "This is interesting. I have always had an unusual fear of heights and of falling. I thought this might have come from a past life, but when I went through the birth experience I became suddenly aware that my fear of falling occurred during the Caesarean section. It was my birth that put this fear into me."

Other subjects who had Caesarean sections expressed a common feeling among all my subjects when the mother was "knocked out" by anesthesia. One subject wrote, "I was pulled from my mother's womb. I was aware of blood around, and intense feelings of loneliness, cold, and bright lights. I was born by Caesarean section. But my greatest feeling right after birth was that I wanted to be held and cuddled by my mother. It wasn't possible for me to do this, because she was anesthetized and simply wasn't there. I felt so very all alone."

Another very interesting subgroup of my subjects were those who had been adopted shortly after birth. Thirty such subjects told me that that was their reason for coming to the workshop. One told me, "I have always wanted to know who my natural mother was and the circumstances of my birth. It has become quite an obsession with me, and I am hoping the hypnosis will help to reveal something that will aid in my search for my mother."

It's interesting that in spite of the great desire consciously to know about their birth, only fourteen of these subjects did experience their births under hypnosis. This means that that group had the same percentage of those experiencing birth as did the group in general. Apparently increased motivation for experiencing birth under hypnosis does not increase the number of subjects who will have the experience. This suggests to me that whether or not people are aware of their birth experience when asked about it under hypnosis does not relate to the conscious wish to know, but instead seems to be regulated by some unconscious decision to permit this information to come into the conscious mind.

Of those adopted subjects who did experience the birth, all but two of them became aware under the hypnosis that they had not known their natural mother or father in a past life, but did have karmic ties with the adoptive parents. Some of these had ties with both adoptive parents, but more commonly they had a tie with one or another (either mother or father) in a past life. This was a surprising result. Those subjects who were looking for their relationship with their natural parents had some unique experiences.

One subject who was searching for her mother became aware under the birth-experience hypnosis that she could hear someone calling her mother's name. The name did not come through with great clarity, but she was quite aware that she was hearing her mother's first name. No other details of the natural mother came through. A number of the subjects who had been adopted responded to the question of whether they were aware of their mother's feelings prior to birth. Almost all of these subjects reported that they were aware that their mother felt great sadness, together with fear.

One subject reported, "I am aware that my mother

feels trapped. She did not want me, but she also knows that she cannot keep me. She feels very tired and sad and simply wants to get the procedure over with."

The karmic ties with the adoptive parents were most interesting. Some of them knew before they were born of the relationship they would have with the adoptive parents, and felt that they would not be able to come to them as their own genetic child but chose the method of adoption as a way to reach their parents. Of course, it can be argued that these subjects probably feel their closest ties with their adoptive parents, so would fantasize this under hypnosis. Nearly all of them wished very much to find out who their natural parents were, but the data that came through was clearly on the mother and father who raised them. If it were fantasy operating, could the unconscious prefer to stay attached to the adoptive parents, and the search for the natural parents be only at a conscious level? However, if we accept these birth experiences as representing a kind of reality, this poses a very interesting question. Is the future ordained? If my subjects knew they would be adopted, then was it all planned ahead of time? If my data is to be accepted as representing reality, then this must be true. Chance and accident apparently played no part in the adoption of my subjects.

One subject, however, had an interesting experience in regard to the adoptive parents. "I chose my parents only for the genetic material they could give me. I chose my adoptive parents and I know ahead of time that I will be adopted by them, because I needed the environment they could provide for me. I had a job to do in this life and I wanted to plan it as carefully as possible. I chose one set of parents for the genetic background, and another for the environment." This subject went through the birth experience twice, and on the second trip more insights came to her. "I became aware that while I was planning my coming lifetime, I had originally chosen to come as a male. I felt that I would choose the body of my brother, eighteen months younger than I, but then I became impatient and decided to come first. I then was in a female body." This subject has always felt uncomfortable as a woman, and felt that the insights she gained under this hypnosis helped to explain to her why she had felt uncomfortable in a woman's body. "I seemed to have goofed on that one," she laughed. "But you know there's a strange thing about this. I was adopted when I was eighteen months old, right after the birth of my brother. We were all up for adoption, and I am not sure at all why I was chosen rather than the newborn. Could it be that I was influencing the adopted parents? I knew before birth that I wanted to be adopted by them. But when I got too eager and came quickly into a female body, apparently I had to arrange things so that I would be adopted instead of the younger brother whom I had originally chosen to be."

Two of the subjects who had been adopted and who had birth experiences did not have the impression that they knew their adoptive parents before they were born. One subject reported, "When you asked if I knew my mother-to-be or father-to-be, I flashed that of course I knew them. They had been children of mine in a past life. In that life I had been quite frivolous and had deserted both of them when they were both young children. I became clearly aware that I was choosing this lifetime in order to experience a feeling of abandonment by my parents. An important part of my life lesson was to be learned here at the beginning; to be thrown onto the sympathies of strangers. I did not know my adoptive parents, I had not known them in past lives. Apparently the only people I knew from a past life were my natural parents. This life was to be an adventurous one, contacting new people, and having new experiences."

The other subject who did not know her adoptive parents had known one natural parent in a past life, the father. "Apparently he did not wish to stay with my mother, and so I was not to know him in this life. He was only there to provide a genetic tie. It's interesting; I seem to have known my husband in a past life and we had been together often. I also knew several close friends, but not my adopted parents."

In summary, my cases of subjects who had been adopted clearly indicated that the circmustances of their natural birth and adoption were known before the lifetime began. These circumstances were chosen just as carefully as other karmic ties to be experienced in the coming lifetime. It is becoming more and more common now for adopted children to seek out their natural parents. Often such seekers tell us that they want to know their physical origins and are very curious about the genetic makeup that only the natural parents could have provided for them. They often try to explain to their adoptive parents that they are not rejecting the adoption and the love they experienced from the adoptive parents, but instead are merely looking to establish where their own physical characteristics came from. Judging from the results of my hypnotic regressions, I think these adopted children are expressing truths.

Our relationships to people in this life do not seem to be based primarily on blood ties. We can feel even closer to a friend than to a brother or sister or parent in this life. Judging from the results on karmic ties under hypnosis, this is because we may have known

these friends much more intimately in past lives than
we have known blood relatives. Blood may be thicker
than water; judging by my results, past-life ties are a
lot thicker than blood.

I had found such interesting agreement among my
subjects on the pre-birth as well as the birth experience, that I started struggling with the question of
how I could possibly validate this material. It seemed
to be obvious that, short of committing suicide and
observing my rebirth, there was no way I could validate the material that came through my subjects. I was
simply running an opinion poll. It was my hope that
I was reaching a subconscious level, rather than a
conscious belief system. But how could I test this? I
did try to rule out all data sheets where the subjects
reported any conscious awareness of the answers to
the questions that came to them. I also tried to rule
out those subjects who seemed not to experience those
elements that suggest to me they are in an altered state
of consciousness and in touch with their subconscious.
For me, the test of this "altered state of consciousness"
that I am calling hypnosis is basically that the time
sense is greatly altered, and my subjects are aware
they are flashing on answers much more rapidly than
they could possibly do in their normal waking consciousness. By those criteria the data sheets I was
working with were as carefully selected as possible.

Was there any other way that I could find out
whether the material I was getting represented conscious beliefs? I knew that opinion polls on spiritual
matters (belief in ESP, interest in and knowledge of
Eastern religious systems, etc.) had been done. Several
of these polls clearly indicated a difference between
subjects queried in the Midwest and subjects on the
West Coast. There seemed to be some cultural dif-

ference here. People in the Midwest were less aware of Eastern spiritual disciplines and generally less interested in ESP.

I decided to run a series of workshops in Minnesota, Illinois, and Michigan to determine if subjects from these areas gave different answers on the birth experience than my subjects in the West had done. I depended on volunteers as I had done on the West Coast. The difference was that most of my West Coast subjects came to me by word of mouth. One subject went to the workshop and told another about it, and then they contacted me. My subjects in the Midwest reported for my sessions through my appearances on radio, television and in newspapers. This suggested to me that I was more likely to get people who were merely curious about the birth experience, in comparison with people on the West Coast, who had already experienced "consciousness raising" workshops. This should result in a difference in the subject's responses under hypnosis, if what I was tapping was merely conscious belief systems.

On the West Coast, a large minority of my subjects had been to Werner Erhard's est training. The processes in est are not significantly different from my hypnotic workshop, so in a way I was tapping at least some subjects who had experienced this before. Also, some of my West Coast subjects had been through the birthing process in therapy-oriented psychology workshops. To my knowledge, none of my Midwestern subjects had been "rebirthed." I also found that very few of my Midwestern subjects had been trained in est, as this particular system has not spread widely to the mid-section of the country. Instead, I found that some of my subjects, again not a majority by any means but a substantial minority, had been through the Silva Mind Control training.

This system of developing awareness of altered states of consciousness was developed in Texas, and apparently is much more widespread than I was aware in the Midwest. Are the Silva Mind Control processes like est and, again, are both like my workshops? Certainly, there are many differences. Neither of these systems refers to the altered state as hypnosis. I have no personal knowledge of either est or Silva Mind Control, but it seems to be clear that the results they are getting are quite similar to mine.

I found that among my Midwestern subjects, many more were involved in what I might call Christian mystic practices, such as prayer groups, than in Eastern religious traditions. On the West Coast, my subjects were more into yoga. In the Middle West the introduction to this field tended to come more through Astrology and through such groups as Spiritual Frontiers Fellowship. When I describe groups as "Christian Mystic Groups," I am speaking here of the charismatic movement among the Catholics, and the many prayer groups that operate within Protestant denominations. As far as I am aware, the Christian consciousness-development techniques are created within the framework of Christian doctrine. But the techniques of the prayer group, whether used for healing or simply as a group meditation process, apparently tap the same state of consciousness as seen in est and Silva Mind Control. The belief systems may be different, but the state of consciousness seems to be the same.

So there were cultural differences between my subjects on the West Coast and my subjects in the Midwest. Although I had expected more naive subjects in the Midwest, I was surprised to find that the groups revealed substantially the same experiences under hypnosis. The belief systems were different; the ways of recruiting subjects were different; the previous training they had received was different, but the results were the same!

I figured up the percentages for my 150 subjects in the Midwest and then compared them with the percentages of my 600 subjects on the West Coast. For example, in response to the question, "Did you choose to be born?" 64 percent of my West Coast subjects said they did, where 62 percent of the Midwest subjects said they had chosen to be born. The figures for the answer "No" for the question, "Did you choose to be born?" were 23 percent for the West Coast group and 29 percent for the Midwest group. An analysis of whether these percentage-point differences are significant revealed that they were not statistically significant. (The measure of significance is based on the number of cases in each sample.) There just didn't seem to be that much difference!

Again, on the question of whether or not others helped them choose to be born, 33 percent of the West Coast cases and 31 percent of the Midwest cases said that others helped them choose to be born. Again the difference of two percentage points was not significant.

Subjects told the same story about the process of getting born, apparently regardless of where they lived, what groups they had studied with, and what their conscious belief systems might be. I thought, "Am I somehow influencing these results? Are people reading my mind, and is that why I'm getting similar responses?" This is one reason I went to the statistical method of analysis. If it is true that hypnotists get what they ask for, this phenomenon needs to be ruled out in any investigation that uses hypnosis. By dividing my subjects' responses into categories, I was able to rule this out. For example, on the question,

"Did you choose to be born?" I had my own ideas on this. I had flashed on my own birth experience, and in my case I was eager to be born. If I were somehow conveying this belief system about birth to my subjects, most of my subjects did not agree with me. They seemed to respond much more reluctantly to the prospect of getting born than had been my own experience. Actually, my own experiences on the birth trip were somewhat different than the majority of my subjects. I did have others helping me choose, which was common for the rest of the group, but my feelings about the coming lifetime were quite happy, and I was most anxious to come down through the birth canal and get going on my life. So if my subjects were reading my mind, they took one look at what my thoughts were and went off on their own track.

I have tried to present to the reader my findings as carefully as I can without intruding my own feelings and attitudes into an evaluation of the data. I wanted the reader to get the answers from the data sheets of my subjects rather than filtering them through my mind. But, of course, I have my opinions, my feelings, and my attitudes regarding this material. Now I can throw off the restraint of the objective, scientific observer and sound off a bit.

IX

"THIS WAS A STRANGE EXPERIENCE!" MY SUBJECTS REPORTED

The people who wrote these data sheets on the answers that flahsed in their heads to my questions were a varied group. They came to the sessions with different religious belief systems and certainly they would not have all agreed on such questions as whether or not they chose to be born. The one thing that characterized them is that they were open to exploring hypnosis and interested in the possibility of reincarnation. In that sense, they apparently had no block based on a current belief system that would keep this information from coming into their mind.

Some of my subjects reported that the impressions they did have were in conflict with their conscious beliefs. "I always thought that fetuses could feel and understand," reported one subject to me. "I was so surprised to find that I wasn't really in the fetus much at all. The strangest part of the experience to me was the feeling that somehow I was helping to create the fetus."

Other subjects who got impressions about the pre-birth experience also expressed amazement about what they had written on their data sheets. A few of these seemed to be using a form of automatic writing, and didn't really know what they had said until they read over the data sheet after they had completed it. Others reported that they were aware of the answers that flashed in their head, but kept fighting them.

"I kept thinking that what I was getting was nonsense, but your questions went on rapidly and I did remember my answers. I had the feeling that if I had time to think over your questions, I might have answered them differently, because they are in conflict with what I do believe." This subject was strongly against abortion, and was surprised to find that the soul or spirit she had been was resistant to being born rather than eager to come into the world.

The great majority of my subjects who expressed their thoughts to me after the experience said that they were quite astonished about what emerged and that it would take some time to digest the experience.

But what of the people who got no impressions? This was a very disappointed group of people. Many of them had hoped for answers to my questions when they found that this would be one of the hypnotic trips in the workshop. Most of them clearly had ideas in advance about whom they had been related to in past lives, and many thought that the birth experience would be easy for them to pick up under hypnosis. This was especially true after the first hypnotic trip when 95 percent of them found that they were flashing on answers to my questions about past lives.

So when many of them found themselves going too deep and waking up from the "birth trip" with no impressions at all, at first I thought this might be because they had already been hypnotized twice and three inductions in a row might have put them too far under. I did some experimentation with several groups, introducing the birth trip first rather than the past-life regressions.

But changing the order of the hypnosis didn't change the results one bit. No matter when I hypnotized them, or how much experience they had had in going under hypnosis, around 52 percent of all my subjects still got no answers on the birth trip. Of the 52 percent not responding, fully 40 percent reported a specific phenomenon as they went deeper into hypnosis. These 40 percent reported that they began to see colors drifting in front of their closed eyelids, as I took them down to the brain-wave level of five cycles per second. There didn't seem to be any one consistent color; each subject seemed to see a slightly different one. But the phenomenon of drifting fields of color was to recur again and again in the hypnosis, especially on this birth trip.

"I see purplish-gray colors fading in and out, then a bright orange," a subject would report. "Then I don't remember anything until I heard your voice say that a golden ball of energy was returning from outer space."

Most of my subjects who did drop into what they call sleep, and into what I call the delta brain-wave state, did hear my voice bringing them out of the hypnosis. If they were deeply asleep and not listening to my voice, how did they know when to awake from the hypnosis? True, a few subjects did not awaken until the lights were turned on in the room, but these were always a very small minority of my sleeping subjects. Indeed at some level they were hearing my voice, but for some reason they were not participating in this particular trip.

I tried to find out what might be causing this. I reasoned that if it were simply the fact that this was their third hypnotic induction, many of them would drop off too deeply to recall even before I got them to remember pictures of themselves in childhood. So I tested this, and found that my sleeping subjects nearly all remembered vividly the pictures of themselves as children. As a matter of fact, some subjects felt that the train of thought these images brought about kept them from going on the birth trip.

"I got so fascinated in thinking about the pictures that the ideas you expressed seemed to stay with me and take me into some strange place. I became aware of just how mysterious I am to myself now, and I kept wondering about the potentials in my past that I had forgotten. And then it all seemed to trail away, and the next thing I remember is hearing your voice count us down to waking up."

Other subjects also experienced the sense of illumination during the time I was asking them to recall the feel of their bodies at age three. It was as though this idea, new to them, absorbed their attention to the exclusion of the rest of my instructions.

Some of my sleeping subjects also seemed to know that there was some mental activity going on during the time when they were asleep.

"Thoughts seemed to come into my mind, and I know I was someplace, but now I just can't remember what I experienced. I didn't seem to be listening to your voice, though," one subject reported to me.

About 12 percent of my subjects on the birth trip said that they lay quietly the whole time, did not go to sleep, heard all my questions, but found that they went blank when it came to answering the questions. Typical of this group was the subject who told me,

"I was so anxious to get answers for this, and I was really eager for it. When you asked the questions, it was as though a white wall came down in my mind. Somehow I knew I just wasn't going to be able to get the answers to your questions. It was as though I went blank." This phenomenon was very interesting to me. I wondered if these subjects were simply tired of being hypnotized and lying on the floor, and therefore were not getting the birth experience even though they had recalled past lives. I didn't know any way to test this, except by reversing the order of the trip. The only result of reversing the order of the trips was that the same percentage still got no answers, though fewer went to sleep.

What was happening here? If past-life recall is fantasy, and if the birth trip is fantasy, why wouldn't one be as easy to get as the other? At least my subjects know they were born into this world, though they may indeed doubt whether they had past lives! Why did just under half of my subjects respond to the birth trip, when 95 percent of my subjects had responded with past-life recall in the same hypnotic workshops?

In discussing this question with the subjects who had experienced the birth and those who got nothing, I sensed a real difference in the two groups. It was as though the people who got the answers were somehow better versed in spiritual matters. Many of them had been in transcendental meditation classes or had meditated on their own or been in prayer groups of some kind. In a sense, it was the veterans of the consciousness movement who tended to get the answers on the birth trips. Was it possible that the answers I was getting to my questions about birth were because of a similar mind-set in people who were experienced in the meditative disciplines? Certainly the belief systems differed in that those who were in Christian prayer groups or meditation groups had a different outlook on theology than those who were veterans of yoga. Was the difference just that some subjects were more experienced in going into their right brain? Or was I tapping some common belief system?

It was hard to come up with a way of testing this. On the one hand I had the hypothesis that maybe what I was getting on the birth trip were the responses of sophisticated subjects who had studied widely and were knowledgeable about inner states of consciousness, so what I was getting was a whole set of beliefs about reincarnation and rebirth from them. Perhaps my less sophisticated subjects who had heard about reincarnation but had done little work themselves in the spiritual disciplines, simply didn't share a common belief system and that was why they were not getting answers to my questions.

Though it isn't possible on the basis of my research to rule out the possibility that my subjects are responding from a common set of conscious beliefs about the between-life state, my discussions with subjects indicated that their conscious beliefs were considerably more diverse than the responses I got under hypnosis. Some of these subjects had been through the birth process in therapeutic workshops, as well as in my research workshop. All of these told me that they had experienced similar phenomenon in moving through the birth canal and on experiencing the world after emerging from the body of the mother, but they said none of them had been asked the questions about pre-birth experience before. Yet the great similarity of their answers to my questions remains.

What often happened in my groups was that after the birth experience, subjects were convinced that

their answers were unique to them, and they wondered why they had come up with this. Most of them
were surprised when I told them that their responses
were typical of those I had obtained before. The subjects who expressed reluctance at being born seemed
especially concerned at their feeling. One subject
told me, "I always thought that it was a privilege to be
in the world, and that I loved to be alive. I was really
shocked to find how reluctant I was to be born. Am I
just peculiar this way?" I assured her that this was a
common finding, and she was both surprised and relieved to hear this.

But the most striking response of all in my subjects
was the depth of emotion expressed during the birth
experience. This requires some careful analysis, and I
hope the reader will go along with me as I try to
explain some of the things I believe I have found
about this altered state of consciousness we have
called "hypnosis." In essence, I feel that the mental
state people are in when they are "hypnotized" is
basically a variant of the sleep state. I have found
that it is easiest to get people in this state by giving
instructions that result in rapid eye movement, which
is the lightest state of our nighttime sleep where
dreams occur. When people are in the dream state,
they seem to be activating the right brain hemisphere.
While the right brain is active in flashing on sensory
memories, something seems to be happening in the
nervous system. The muscles are very relaxed, indicating that there is little adrenalin flowing through
the system, and that the body has relaxed its normal
state of vigilance. The reaction to outside stimuli is
reduced, and the mind seems focussed on the voice
(or thoughts!) of the hypnotist. When the muscles of
the body are relaxed, the right brain seems unusually
sensitive to cues coming from the internal body organs.

Some of my subjects report being aware of their heartbeat and have given me other reports indicating to me that they are highly responsive and emotionally reactive, both in terms of feelings coming into their awareness, and in terms of internal body-organ responses to these feelings.

I was struck by the similarity between this state and the state we are in when we dream. Many of us can recall the strong emotional feelings we have experienced in dreams, and even the physical responses to this when we awaken. It may be that what we experience as "nightmares" are actually dream situations, in which the body system is so aroused that it switches from the concentration on the internal organs to a quick flush of adrenalin that brings the muscular-skeletal nervous system into high reactivity. This is probably why we awaken from such dreams, and tend to remember them more than we remember those that occur that do not have frightening content. It seems that when adrenalin rushes through our body, increasing the heart rate and tensing the muscle systems, it brings us into left-brain awareness. When we are functioning in our left brain, we are what we call "awake."

So when frightening dreams wake us, the *way* in which they wake us seems to be by switching the internal blood supply and nervous system from the internal organs to the skeletal muscular system. The emotion of fear seems to be that which triggers this adrenalin response that wakes us from our sleep.

This "flight or fight" adrenalin response system is well known and has been carefully studied in laboratories. What we haven't done is apply this knowledge to the states of consciousness that in our culture we normally refer to as "sleep."

If indeed I was exploring a variation of the sleep

state when I put my subjects on the floor, told them to close their eyes and concentrate on my questions, and got them into rapid eye movement, then this gave me an interesting opportunity to check some aspects of the emotions we have in dreams. I had found earlier in my therapeutic practice that the dreams relating to fear were very close to the surface and were easy for my patients to recall. Dreams where the emotions were more diffuse or pleasant required more effort on the part of my patients to remember them and bring them into the therapy session. It was interesting to note that my subjects who fell into the deeper sleep states under the hypnotic workshop conditions almost always awoke with pleasant feelings. In part this was because I suggested to them that they would feel remarkably good when they awoke, but the experience went deeper than simply following the hypnotist's instructions.

I myself tend to go into deep sleep states when I hear my own voice on tape hypnotizing. I have noticed that when I take these restorative naps while listening to my own tapes, I am able to recall only fragments of what I am experiencing. Almost always I seem to be experiencing a floating feeling, preceded by images from my current life. The emotions I awake with seem to be part and parcel of what I am experiencing while "deeply asleep." In comparing the experience of taking a sound nap while listening to a hypnotist's voice, to the experience of taking a forty-minute catnap in the middle of the day, it's obvious that the hypnotic nap is a lot more refreshing. My own impression from my own experience is that this is because in the usual catnap situation my mind is busy dealing with current problems which are often expressed in dream symbols. Under the hypnotic condition, I seem to drift to deeper states and the dream experiences are both more diffuse and definitely more pleasant.

The experience of deep sleep under hypnosis as very refreshing and pleasant is confirmed by nearly all of my subjects. They may feel angry in a sense because they have "missed" the hypnotic trip, but the need to experience this profoundly pleasant and relaxing state often overcomes the conscious wish to follow my voice and go on the hypnotic trip. This phenomenon is so marked that I spend much of my time when my subjects are under hypnosis in getting them to "wake up to my voice and just to my voice" than in getting them into the rapid-eye-movement state. I have even been known to say, when my subjects are under hypnosis and I am aware that they are deeply asleep, "You paid good money for this hypnotic session, so now you will attend to my voice and be able to respond to my questions!" I also tell my subjects that no matter how deeply and pleasantly asleep they may be, when they hear my voice say the word "now" they will awaken to my voice. Most subjects do report that they become aware of my voice saying the word "now," but that they quickly drift back into the pleasant place where they are no longer responding to me.

What exactly *is* this pleasant state? My subjects are as baffled in trying to respond to this as I am. "I don't know where I was, but it sure was pleasant," most subjects report. So the emotions that are activated in the deep sleep in my hypnotic workshops are pleasant ones. What of the unpleasant ones?

My long training as a psychotherapist made me aware that most of the things that we "forget" are unpleasant episodes in the past that we would prefer not to remember. Freud's great insight, described by him in his book, *The Psychopathology of Everyday*

Life, was that we tend to forget dentist appointments much more quickly than we forget invitations to parties. Traumatic incidents from our past are usually buried, and it is well and good that this is so. We are busy enough in the course of the ordinary day with the challenges and excitments of everyday living, without spending much time dwelling on sad experiences in the past. Of course, most psychotherapeutic systems accept the idea that if the trauma is severe enough we may be able to consciously forget it, but its effects will still be operative in the subconscious and will cause the development of neurotic symptoms in an attempt to continue to control the unpleasant emotions that stem from the trauma.

This is the reason why such techniques as hypnosis can be dangerous. Our subconscious lies open and responsive to questioning and it is quite possible that very disturbing incidents in the past will rise up into conscious awareness during the altered state we call hypnosis. Certainly we all know that our dreams at night do reflect past trauma. Soldiers returning from Vietnam very frequently report continuous disturbing dreams about their experience. It is as though when we suffer a severe trauma, we may block it from our conscious awareness but the dreaming self continues to work on the problem in an attempt to come to some terms with it.

Because the possibility is always there that my subjects will run across unhappy emotions, I feel it is very important to turn over control of this memory recall to the subconscious of each individual subject. I instruct them that their subconscious will immediately remove them from the recall of any disturbing material, and I find that this works very well indeed. My subjects do find themselves suddenly drifting into a deep sleep, or switching to another

series of images in another past life, when they hit
upon disturbing emotions in a specific past-life recall.
I also tell my subjects that if the death experience
becomes uncomfortable in any way, they will find
themselves removed from that situation. Some subjects go into deep sleep at this point and no longer
hear my questions. They are usually surprised to
find that this "deep sleep" occurred at the moment I
was instructing them to avoid any unpleasant emotion.
Apparently, the conscious mind is not aware of the
expected trauma if the regression continues, but the
subconscious is and responds immediately to my suggestion.

I have found these safeguards to be indispensable
in my hypnotic workshops. I have heard reports from
therapists, and also from groups which have experi-
mented in a casual way with the phenomenon of past-
life recall, that subjects have been taken into such
traumatic experiences that it has affected them for
months. It is as though there is buried material that
emerges into conscious awareness in the hypnotic situation, then continues to obsess the subject. And they
experience many dreams about the trauma, and their
everyday working consciousness is also invaded with
memories, confusions and awareness of feelings. Of
course, this is not always a negative effect. Just as
people in therapy can become aware of an incident
in their childhood which is causing fears and phobias
now, so subjects who have encountered traumas in
past-life recall are then able to work them through in
the conscious state. As in therapy, this takes time.
It also takes a sympathetic, understanding and patient
therapist to deal with the emotions uncovered under
the hypnotic recall.

To work on one's own inner feelings is always a
difficult task, avoided by most of us in the interests

of maintaining our everyday efficiency. But what of the emotions I encountered in my subjects when I took them to the birth experience? There is a current school of thought in psychotherapy that reliving one's birth is therapeutic. When subjects are taken to the birth experience, most of the emotions encountered are negative. Arthur Janov calls this the "primal scream." Do we indeed come screaming into the world? Is the origin of many of our feelings of insecurity and unhappiness the experience of being thrust rudely into the physical world?

If you read this far into this book, you are aware of how reluctant most of my subjects were to take on the task of living in the physical universe. Certainly there are negative feelings involved in this. Were my subjects who went into deep sleep avoiding the pain of the birth experience?

In an attempt to answer this question, I used a different technique on several groups. After having them look at the pictures of themselves in childhood, and taking them on the trip "out of their bodies," I then asked them to flash the answer to this question:

"Are you ready to discover your experiences before birth? The answer yes or the answer no will flash in your mind." The responses to this were interesting. Some subjects did flash the answer "no" and then went into a deep sleep. Other subjects reported that they got the answer "yes and no," parts of the experience are available for you to recall, but other parts are not for you to know yet. One subject reported to me, "And then when you went on with the questions, I was aware that it was all right for me to remember the experience of being born, but I flashed that I was not supposed to recall the experience before birth. Somehow I felt I wasn't ready yet."

Those subjects who flashed the answer "yes" did get

the answers to my questions, and it is apparently this group who are reporting the experiences described in this book. They somehow did have permission from their subconscious to recall this. It's interesting to note that several subjects who repeated my workshops found that more information came to them on the second time they went through the birth trip than on the first. It was as though more of their awareness had opened up for them in the intervening months between workshops.

"The first time I went to the birth experience, I got some answers about what it was like to be born. But I didn't get much information about who I knew in previous lives, or why I was here this time. Going through it the second time, more answers came into my mind. Actually, since the first hypnotic workshop I have been having some interesting dreams about the past lives that flashed in my mind. In these dreams, the karmic ties I had with people in my life now seem to come more clearly to my mind. Maybe that's why I'm getting the birth experience now."

One of the most striking things about the birth trip was the response of my subjects as they awoke from the hypnosis. They all had a faraway look in their eyes. After the first two trips, my subjects were often full of questions they wanted to discuss with me. After the birth trip, people looked remarkably thoughtful and subdued, and I seldom got many questions. Perhaps one reason for this was that so many subjects had fallen into the deep sleep state. But it was obvious that those who had gotten the impressions and were filling out their data sheets seemed very quiet. I began to explore this phenomenon by asking what had happened to them on the birth trip.

"It's very hard to describe," one subject explained to me. "I have very strong emotional feelings, but they're not easy to explain. I feel as though I have been on a very long journey into a strange part of my mind. My major emotion was not that of fear, which I had sort of expected. I didn't look forward to the actual birth, moving down the birth canal, because I thought it would be physically painful. But it wasn't that I had any pain.

"No, the experience was more one of deep compassion. I felt compassion not only for the infant who was me, but for my mother and indeed everyone in the delivery room. It was as though I was leaving a beautiful, brightly-lit place where many things were open to me, to come down into a very closed and puzzling environment. It seemed as though I knew all of the troubles that lay ahead, and I felt that it was such a waste that we humans don't understand."

My subject laughed a little, saying, "I know that sounds strange, even to me. Don't know or understand *what?* Well, when I was under the hypnosis, it seemed so clear to me, that to be alive in the body is to be isolated from our true selves and away from the true knowledge that's available to us when we are not in a body. I knew it was necessary to go through the experience of this life, but I'm not sure why. Yet, it seemed such a tragedy that my mother, the doctor, and others had no real understanding of what life is. This came through crystal-clear to me under the hypnosis."

Many other subjects expressed much the same sentiments to me. Some reported, "Actual tears were running down my cheeks as you asked us to come to the time of decision about being born. It isn't so much sadness, because I don't feel sad now that I'm awake. It just—well, it's too routine. Life in a body is rough."

Other subjects told me that they were very quiet and thoughtful because of the insights that came to them on this hypnotic trip about their relationships in their current lives. "I became so clearly aware on this hypnotic trip of my karmic tie to my mother. I have never understood the rejection she has felt toward me, but now I feel I do understand it. I did come in a body in this life in order to make up to her for things I had done to her in a past life, and to help her understand and awaken."

Another subject told me, "Now I understand why I have always been so frightened of my father. It's not really anything he has done in this life, but I guess I always feared he would do to me in this life what he did to me in a past life. I understand now that the problem is not so much with my father, but with my fear of him. It is as though I can't learn to trust until I learn to overcome the fears I had because of what happened in a past lifetime."

Other subjects found it hard to discuss their experiences. It seemed to be easy for them to talk about their past-life recall, but the material that emerged on the birth trip seemed somehow too personal. It also had a quality of intellectual profundity that baffled some of my subjects. "I felt such compassion for the infant who was me, and this seemed strange to me. I still don't understand it, but I'm filled with emotion now and I don't want to talk about it. I don't feel bad, it's not that. There is no fear involved, no grief. It's as though a sense of enlightenment has come over me. I know I will never forget this experience."

Many other subjects who did get answers to the birth trip echoed the sentiments of the subject above. Of all the regressions, it was the birth trip that seemed most enlightening to them. Some of these subjects have contacted me later and told me that the experience profoundly changed their lives. They felt that flashing on their purpose made it much easier for them to understand their lives and to live each moment with more warmth and compassion for others around them. Others said they had a stronger sense of their purpose now, and found new directions opening for them. Several others told me that the major result of having been in a workshop and having experienced the birth trip was that they felt more open to their subconscious minds.

"I see now that I was thinking of myself in a much too narrow and restricted sense. I feel in touch now with my dreaming self, as well as my waking self. I don't take the happenings of every day with such seriousness as I did before. It's as though I have a different perspective now each day of my life, and more of an inner serenity in dealing with the ups and downs that are inevitable."

While it is very gratifying to hear these experiences of my subjects, I feel that the broadening of self-awareness that they have experienced after the workshop is part of their own development and not due to anything I might have said or done. I have the strong feeling that people were drawn to my workshop because they were at a certain point in their lives where they were ready and open for new experiences. They used my hypnotic inductions, my questions, my suggestions, as a way to open up. Some other experience could have served just as well to bring them to this self-awareness; I don't feel it's a magic within my hypnotic workshops. It's a magic within my subjects, ready to unfold.

As I listened to my subjects' explanations of the changes in their life, I thought once more of my image of the tightly budded rose opening. No rose can open until it has reached a certain stage; the fragrance is locked inside the bud until the petals have grown to a certain size. Then one day, when the sun shines very brightly, the petals are ready to respond to the warmth and then they do indeed open. Is the magic in the sun? The magic lies in the rose itself, in its slow formation, in its gradual unfolding. When a rose is ready to open, it draws to itself the sunshine.

X

FINDING TRUTH ON THE ALL-AMERICAN TALK SHOW

It is with some trepidation that I offer this book to the reader. I have tried to be as honest as I can in describing how I collected the data, and in giving the reader the exact words of my subjects in response to my questions. But I know this is, in media lingo, a hot topic. My research is bound to be controversial and I know it will be criticized by many.

If the public expresses its interest in the subject of this book, I know I will be contacted by talk show hosts. They will "pencil me in" for a show to push my book. I know how these things go. An interviewer who hasn't had time to read the book and is concerned with an offer he just got to go to another station, hurriedly introduces himself to me just before the cameras swing around to us.

"Tell me what your book is about." He smiles at me.

How on earth am I to tell him? "Oh," I comment, "it's about where we are when we're not alive and how we choose to come into this life. It's about people we've known in past lives and how they are related to us now. It's about what the baby experiences when it emerges into the cold light of the delivery room. It's about life, death and the meaning of it all."

The interviewer smiles at me and looks a bit puzzled. "Could you tell me more?" he asks.

I begin. "Well, I had hypnotized over two thousand subjects in group hypnotic workshops."

"What are group hypnotic workshops?" the interviewer asks.

Just as I'm about to answer, a commercial comes on for dog food. When finally we turn from the commercial to my segment of the program, the interviewer repeats his question.

"Can you hypnotize people in groups? I thought you could only hypnotize people one at a time," he remarks to me.

I start to answer him, and a table full of health food is wheeled in just outside of camera range. A lady from the local health food store busily begins preparing the dish that will be described in the next segment of the program. The talk show host looks distracted for a moment, then turns to me again.

"Well, it's been delightful talking with you, and I'm sure we all learned a lot."

"Well, thank you. It was good to be here," I smile weakly.

After a few more such interviews on local stations around the country, word of my subject hits the media in New York. The producer of a late-night talk show, looking through the newspapers in the hope of getting some guest who isn't a Hollywood celebrity who will bore everyone to death with his latest movie, runs across an article on my work. The newspaper reporter has quoted experts in the field who claim I couldn't possibly have hypnotized 2,000 people.

"Hey, Marcia, I think I got an idea for that slot Saturday night two weeks from now. We can get together a group of guests and let them argue out the business of reincarnation. Reincarnation always gets good ratings."

Marcia, his assistant, is somewhat doubtful. "We had a show on Astrology last month," she complains. "You know we said we were only going to have these kooky topics once every two months."

"Well, it's a hot subject now, so let's have another one now. Get on the horn and see if you can invite about six guests. Get a head of some psychiatrists' association and someone from the Ethical Hypnosis Society, too, who knows what he's talking about when it comes to hypnosis. I guess we oughta have that gal from Anita Bryant's organization who says she wants to present the Christian point of view on talk shows. She's good-looking and we need her for balance."

The producer looks at the newspaper story again. "Oh, Marcia, get that guy from the Committee to Investigate Claims for the Paranormal. I think they got a PR office somewhere here in New York. You know, they're associated with the Humanists Society. We need some guy from their organization, too."

"I think we also need somebody who has been hypnotized by her," Marcia responds. "You know it's always good to have somebody talk about their experiences. These arguments get boring after a while, and you need somebody who can tell what it's really like."

"Okay, Marcia, set it all up. Get this woman from California here to talk about her book."

I get the phone message from New York requesting

me to appear on the talk show. I've watched it several times, and have noticed that the bored-looking host is always careful to represent what he feels to be the popular side of any question. You don't know what he really thinks, but he always seems wide-eyed as he asks questions he thinks the ordinary person would ask. He appears to prefer a slightly macho, sophisticated approach.

My associate, Leona Lee, who handles all the hundreds of details of arranging workshops and seeing that I get my letters written and my appointments met, tells me that I should go. "I know you don't like to travel, and I know how you feel about TV interviews, but they're going to give you two hours. There'll be a chance to discuss this with someone from the Psychiatric Association, the Society for Ethical Hypnosis, and the Committee to Investigate Claims of the Paranormal. I think it's something you ought to do," she tells me.

I'm hesitant. I know that in the past someone who came out with new evidence for any new concept faced a lot of flack from the society he lived in. Galileo got in a lot of trouble, Mesmer was investigated and thrown out of Paris for his work with original hypnosis. Wilhelm Reich got sent to jail by the government for devising and selling orgone boxes, something that's now being investigated seriously. A talk show seemed a very mild way to deal with this. Society was improving in the way it treated new ideas. Now it seemed they got trivialized to death, or talked to death, rather than being subject to solemn procedures by the proper Establshment, as they were in past times. I agreed to go.

I arrived in New York, prepared from sad experience for the incredibly awkward job of getting from Kennedy Airport to Manhattan. The smells of diesel engines and car exhausts, the clutter of luggage, the harsh accents of the New Yorkers fell familiarly on my ear. It took guts and stable nerves to wend one's way around this queen city of the United States. My metabolism began to speed up from its lazy California pace to meet the challenges of moment-by-moment maneuvering in the most exciting city in the world.

As I rode through the streets of Manhattan, memories came sharp and vivid to my mind. I remembered the New York of the 1940's, with its exciting mix of cultural events. Paul Robeson playing *Othello;* Katharine Cornell in Chekhov's *The Cherry Orchard,* the Philharmonic, the Metropolitan Museum. I was young then, and I drank my fill at the cultural fountain of New York, right after World War II. It seemed as though all the culture of Western Civilization had focused here on this twenty-four-square-mile island, as Europe, exhausted from its internal struggles, sent its refugees to our shores. New York stood then as the storehouse and powerhouse of what was left of a civilization that had conquered the world, invented technology, and set mankind on the path of rationalism and its offspring, Science. Back in the '40's, the flow of gold from the banks and treasure houses of Europe had already slid into the subterranean tunnels below Wall Street. America! We were a democracy, we believed in freedom, and yet here we were, the last and most powerful representative of Western European Imperialism. I just enjoyed its fruits back in the '40's, unaware of the tide of history that would move the city from its heyday of power, energy and triumph to its fortress-like nature now.

The fruits of empire made New York rich and glamorous. But as it became a center with a bank on every corner, a center for money and power and glitter and excitement, it drew like a magnet the tides of third-world peoples into its orbit. The natives of Puerto Rico and of Mexico began moving up from Central America to this bastion of power and privilege. The slaves we had imported to this colony grew and multiplied and bought bus tickets from the South to the North. The city was still alive with change and the prospects of adventures to come when I knew it in the 1960's.

I remember that Easter Sunday in the late 1960's when I brought my daughter and niece to the Methodist Church in Greenwich Village to celebrate Easter. We marched out of the church with banners we had made, proclaiming peace, protesting the war, and urging the common spirit of love and humanity. It all seemed so possible then. We moved up to Central Park and joined the "Love-In." The musical *Hair* had just begun its run Off Broadway, and the sparkling April sun made Central Park a magical place to be. New ideas were fermenting and developing, new hope for a merger of all those who sought to share their common humanity calling out in triumph against the backgrounds of the concrete canyons of power and money that is New York.

But all that was gone now, as fleeting as a dream. As I entered the building where the talk show was to take place, two security guards met me at the door. It was necessary to present identification, to sign in and to be escorted to the elevators. Fortress America! I remembered the arguments about isolationism in the late 1930's and thought with wry amusement that we had indeed become isolated, but not as a fortress America against the rest of the world, but as people with money protected by hired guards against the crush of humanity that surrounded Manhattan island now. Crime, the instant Communism in the barrios and the ghettos, threatened these bastions of media power.

When I reached the studio, I was led through the maze of wires and cables to the set for the talk show. It was familiar to me now; the echoing cavern of the studio, the small, brightly-lit area made to look like a comfortable living room. I saw the cameras and the cables as the eyes and ears of millions of people trained upon our small group. I thought how the sensory revolution, begun by the discovery of wave frequencies and the possibility of transmitting sensory messages first through cable and then through transmitters and receivers, had speeded up the changes in our society at a dizzying pace. It took a hundred years for technology to remake the countryside and the cities. It took only fifty years for the revolutions of radio and television to make of us all now one interconnected unit. Maybe this was why history seemed to be speeded up, like a movie film cranked ever faster by some mad technician. Britain had remained on top of the Imperial heap for a hundred years. It looked like our turn as king of the hill would last only from 1940 to 1980. While we lengthen our physical life by medical discoveries, we seem to be shortening the lives of our cultures.

I was introduced to the other panel members, and I looked at them closely. These were slated to be my adversaries in an intellectual argument about the nature of man. Could I guess what they would say?

The man representing the Committee to Investigate Claims of the Paranormal was a big, shaggy guy with rumpled hair. Though I knew he felt the most contempt for my research claim that people remembered the time before birth, I felt an instant liking for him. I had known others like him in my youth. He had spent hours arguing radical politics in the coffee shop at New York University in his early years, learning the fierce debating tactics of New York intellectuals. I knew he prided himself on seeing the world clearly, without illusions. I knew he had taught at various state universities for the past fifteen years, and I know that the '60's had been rough on him. The methods of thought he had learned so well in his youth, the debating tactics, the application of logic to all human situations, the clear-eyed appraisal of the society he prided himself on were no longer interesting to his students. His carefully reasoned arguments in the classroom were now often met by students who challenged the value of science, claiming that it polluted the world. His students were going around singing silly songs, indulging in an emotionalism that he had learned was suspect. Now his students were following various gurus, dropping acid and seeing God. Angrily, he concluded that the pursuit of hallucinations was taking precedence over the reasoned search for knowledge. Reincarnation indeed! How silly can you get! Oh, he thought, the world is hard enough. He had been in psychoanalysis for five years, so he understood the power of irrationality in himself. But he'd be damned if he'd see society carried away on a tide of womanish hysteria over such remnants of the occult as astrology and reincarnation.

When he heard about the Committee to Investigate the Paranormal, he joined eagerly. Here was a chance to bring America back to its senses, to end this sudden uprush of foolishness.

In the back of his mind was the memory of what his father had told him of the plight of the Jews in Poland. The superstitious Christians of that era believed all kinds of wild stories about the Jews. "The Jews eat babies!" His father, with sad wisdom, concluded that if ideas of this religious kind became popular in the neighborhood, a pogrom would result.

Unreasoning superstition was a fearful enemy. The professor felt that the dark night of the soul could arise in America, too, if you weren't constantly vigilant. He didn't oppose people's rights to practice their religion, but he was sure worried when wild ideas began to influence lots of people. Unreason might again lead to the slaughter of the innocents.

The representative of the Christian Council for the Preservation of Family Life, a sweet-faced young woman, smiled nervously at me as we were introduced. I felt I had known her for many years. She came from an area near my family home in the deep South, and I thought I knew how her mind worked. She was a good woman, who did no harm to anyone, and was always gracious to everyone around her. Her religion was a deeply held belief, and I saw how it worked in her life. She felt that she had accepted the living Christ as her savior, and was warmed by the feeling of love this thought gave her. She didn't know or understand much about theological arguments and didn't care. For her, the Bible was Authority and it was all she needed to live a good Christian life. When people argued that the Bible was a book written by man, and contained historical inaccuracies, their arguments simply didn't interest her. The feelings of love and satisfaction she got from the practice of her religion were proof enough to her that Jesus was the Way. She believed in the traditional role of women in the family, and was able to successfully ignore the occasional falls from Christian grace on the part of the male members of her family. That hatred, bigotry and a savage determination to eliminate those who opposed you could also be a part of the social group she was trying to preserve had little meaning for her. If you just held to the word of the Bible, if you accepted the living Jesus, then all these other problems would somehow work themselves out.

When she read the newspapers or watched television she was convinced again of the truth of Billy Graham's sermon, "The Armageddon is coming." The forces of good and evil were obviously fighting for dominance in the United States. The new sexual styles of living, the irreverence toward the church, the new ideas argued by the young people, were all evidence that the End was near.

All these heathenish Eastern religious cults were especially disturbing to her. All the chanting, incense, and TV programs on yoga really confused her. They all probably led to immorality and the destruction of family life.

And now people were talking about this thing called reincarnation. Why do people get so confused and take up these outlandish ideas? You were born, you lived your life as best you could, and when you died there was a judgment as to whether you would go to Heaven or Hell. She felt that her work with the Christian Family Life Institute would help preserve her place in Heaven. Where in the Bible did it say anything about people being born again, except in the blood of the lamb?

But she smiled at me, wondering if I was working for the forces of the devil. I had used hypnosis and everybody knew that you had to be careful when you used anything like hypnosis. The devil lay in wait for unsuspecting souls, and possession by evil spirits was certainly not unknown. Was that what I was doing when I was hypnotizing people? Were my subjects being possessed and the devil using this to put out false ideas like reincarnation?

Next to be introduced to me was the Chairman of

the Committee of the American Psychiatric Association to Evaluate Current Research in Psychodynamics. He was dressed exceedingly well, and he had a sophisticated, at-home air about him as he sat in the television studio. He obviously was a veteran of many committee meetings and news conferences and felt comfortable in his role. I knew he would give me the Establishment psychiatric view of what my subjects were experiencing, and I also knew that he was probably analyzing my motives as well. He reminded me of many psychiatrists I had known in the hospitals where I had worked. They were skilled at committee meetings, very good at tossing around words, and their basic job was to soothe all the participants in any committee meeting and to arrive at a neatly worded concensus. I thought I had him pegged right away.

But I was wrong. The good doctor was going through a critical time in his own life now. His children, who had gone to all the proper universities, were challenging all his beliefs. He had provided the obligatory home in Westchester, with its pseudo-rural white fences, but he had to drive into the city to chair his committee meetings. There was a kind of emptiness inside the good doctor, as he had begun to see his life as having less and less meaning. Perhaps the kids were right. Maybe you ought to get a farm in Vermont and forget all the hassles. He was making good money, but somehow it was never enough. More and more he was using the money he earned to escape from the city and its environs, looking for a more peaceful way of life. He had begun to doubt the assumptions that had ruled his professional life, and actually he had an intense curiosity about my work.

The next panel member greeted me with icy politeness. He was a small man, with a mustache and an air of controlled hostility. He represented the Society for the Promotion of Ethical Hypnosis, and I wondered where he stood on the issues. I was to find out that he was dominated by a fear that a very useful therapeutic tool, hypnosis, was being dragged once again into the arena of public entertainment. For twenty years he had fought to keep stage magicians from employing this tool in frivolous ways, and now he found the professionals were beginning to use it for such outlandish things as regressing people to the before-birth experience. Indeed! How on earth could the fetus talk to the hypnotist? It all seemed to him to be a tremendous back-sliding from the pinnacle of respectability hypnosis had finally reached. It was beginning to be accepted as a therapeutic tool, and now this!

The last panel member was someone I hadn't seen for two years. I had regressed him in a hypnotic workshop when I was on the East Coast in 1976. He smiled at me, and I began to remember his experience under hypnosis. He had been one of my better subjects; his experiences were vivid and expressed in bodily movements as well as thoughts. He had had a particularly interesting birth experience, and he told me later that it had given him a deep insight into his own being. I hoped that the controversy of the talk show would not disturb the serenity he felt he had achieved after the hypnosis.

And then the free-for-all began. "Do you call this hypnosis, laying a bunch of people on the floor and talking to them?"

"Well, I tried to use objective criteria for the altered state of consciousness we call hypnosis. I believe that what we call hypnosis is actually a right brain . . ."

I was interrupted by the lady from the Christian Family Foundation, "But don't you think that tampering with people's beliefs is harmful to them?"

"Well, I didn't feel I was tampering with their beliefs. I was just asking the questions to see if all my subjects would reach some kind of agreement on . . . "

"But don't you think most people want to believe there's an afterlife? We are all afraid of death, and we imagine all these pleasant things because . . . "

The man from the Committee to Investigate the Paranormal was interrupted by the psychiatrist.

"On the other hand, don't you feel that perhaps people are regaining the oceanic feeling the infant experiences as described by Freud in . . . "

"Well, there was some of that in my experience," the young subject of mine responded. "But it was closer to what I had in meditation using the yoga techniques of . . . "

"Yoga! Then this is not really hypnosis, it is just another religious system." The man from the Committee to Support Ethical Hypnosis smiled triumphantly.

"Well, you see," I gamely entered the fray once more, "it has something in common with certain religious systems, I'll agree to that. But the experience seems to transcend particular religious beliefs. People seem to be reporting the same phenomena regardless of what their . . . "

"But who is reporting this? How can the infant report anything when it doesn't know English yet?" interposed the gentleman from Ethical Hypnosis.

"It seems to be an observing higher self that is reporting on the experiences, not the fetus or infant himself," I answered him. "Ernest Hilgard, Director of the Hypnotic Institute at Stanford University, has noted that there seems to be an observer who is aware of pain even though the hypnotized subject reports feeling no pain." I was pleased to have gotten in a complete sentence.

"Would you consider this observer to be the super-ego? Or is it the ego?" asked the psychiatrist.

The lady from the Christian Family Foundation interjected a comment, "Of course, we all have a soul. And that soul joins Jesus. I don't see anything in your book about Jesus."

I turned to the lady from the Christian Family Foundation and tried to explain. "Well, I didn't ask about specific religious figures," I began. "People did seem to experience great love and compassion, and some of them described a white light that seemed filled with love. Perhaps this is the Jesus image . . . "

"Where was God?" asked the lady seriously.

My subject came to my rescue. "To me, when I was hypnotized, it didn't seem as though there were a simple, God-like person, instead it seemed as though there were a group of other people helping me choose to be born. Some were wiser than others, but there didn't seem to be one person or one entity controlling the process."

The psychiatrist interjected, "Of course, the infant has not had time to establish yet the hierarchal father figure that later becomes the concept of God."

The gentleman from the Committee to Investigate the Paranormal had been looking increasingly disgusted at this interchange. He broke in, "Can't you see it's all a lot of wishful thinking? Sure, we all want to believe that we survive death. We don't want to face the reality that we are alone in the universe, so we make up UFO's, we make up heavens. We tell ourselves pretty stories so we don't have to face the truth."

This brought up a general melee of conversation. "I certainly didn't make up Jesus!" angrily stated the woman from the Christian Family Foundation.

"I don't think it was wishful thinking I was feeling while I was hypnotized," said the subject.

"I don't see how all this enters into the question of whether it was hypnosis or not. This lady has not hypnotized anyone, she has merely talked them into giving her answers that she wanted to hear," angrily interjected the gentleman from Ethical Hypnosis.

The psychiatrist joined in. "Now, I think we can all reach agreement on this if we just sit down and examine our positions. Certainly we have here a variety of beliefs, but there must be some things in common that we all believe."

The talk show host, whose job has been made easy by the vigor of the conversation, broke in, taking advantage of the lull the psychiatrist's soothing words had spread. "Now if I understand it right, all your subjects said that they had known people in past lives that were now in their present life? How did they know this?" he asked me.

"Well, I just asked if they were aware of how they knew these persons. I don't know how they got the answers myself. I just know they gave the answers."

The talk show host looked unconvinced. "But *how* do you know if you've known people in past lives?"

My subject intervened again, saying, "It just flashes in your mind. It's like when you're in a dream and you're riding in a car with someone in the dream and they look like Bette Davis, but you really know it's your grandmother."

"Dream!" The gentleman from the Committee to Investigate the Paranormal looked triumphant. "So you admit that all this in the book is just people's dreams. We all know that dreams are hallucinations."

"But what are hallucinations?" I asked, glad to get a word in again. "If only one person sees something and the people around them don't, we call that an hallucination. But my subjects all seem to be hallucinating roughly the same thing. When does a joint hallucination become reality? It seems to me that what we call reality is what other people agree with us about," I went on.

"Well I certainly don't agree that people are born again over and over," chimed in the lady from the Christian Family Foundation. "We go to God. Where is God in your study? Don't we meet Jesus when we die?"

"Well . . . " And soon it was time to end the discussion. No one had changed their mind. We all left the studio with the same impressions and belief systems that we had arrived with.

The only exception to this was Marcia, the producer's assistant. She had been standing to one side of the set, clutching her clipboard and listening to us. As she listened, an incident she had forgotten popped back into her mind. Three years before her father had died. She awoke in the middle of the night and saw him clearly standing by her bed. She saw his face as clearly as she would have at any other time. She knew it was he. He had smiled lovingly at her and then somehow just disappeared. Later that day she received word that he had died of a heart attack, at exactly the moment she had seen him in her bedroom. This experience was disturbing to her sense of what was normal and proper. It did help her through her grief process, because at some level she knew that her father would live on. But she hadn't wanted to examine it or think about it. It was a hallucination! But why that hallucination just at that moment? As memory of the incident flooded back into her mind, she decided that she simply must explore this further. Perhaps there was much more to life and death than she had dreamed of. Her search began.

And so we all went home, to dream, to hallucinate, each in our own way. For sixteen of the twenty-four hours we had considered ourselves alert, awake, functioning people in a busy world. But all of us spent eight hours with our body lying quietly in a bed, and our mind roaming the fields of consciousness beyond the level of awareness our ego could comprehend.

I dream too. And this is my dream.

I seem to be standing somewhere in the presence of an entity whose thoughts were exchanged easily with me. My guide or mentor told me, "See your body lying down there on that bed in that New York motel room? A part of your energy, your awareness, is maintaining the cellular structure of that body. But the rest of your consciousness is up here now with me. You're not having images, or flashing on pictures and scenes, because now you are in a deeper state than rapid eye-movement sleep. Your brain waves are now functioning at around four cycles per second, and you are in a deep place where I can be in touch with you."

"Who are you?" I "thought" to him.

"I am a part of yourself. A part of yourself that knows more than that portion of your consciousness that thinks it lives in that body down there. I'm here to comfort and console you, to guide and direct you, through that little play you call *Being Alive on Earth*. You consult with me every night, as you do with other parts of your personality, and together we plan and direct your activities on earth."

"But aren't I on earth now? Am I in heaven?"

"No, there is no heaven, no hell, no other place. This is your natural home, the home of your consciousness. We don't know time or space here. Here only thought is reality."

"But how come I have a body? The world is real enough, it has mountains and oceans, seasons and years. Are you telling me that all that is not real?"

"Of course, it is real, because you and the others who are alive with you agree that it is real. You see, you all create your own realities. And as a group those consciousnesses who have decided to act out a play called *Being Alive on Earth* have devised a set of stage directions. Your stage directions are very real to you. Right now you have stepped off into the wings of a stage set, which is why you are able to talk with me now. When your alarm clock rings in the morning, you will once more take your place on the stage and act out the drama which you have created. The painted scenery will be real to you, and your fellow actors even more real to you. And yet, in a way, you are all figments of your own imagination."

"But I don't understand!" I protested. "How are you going to know what's real? It's necessary that you have some common sense about this if you're going to lead a decent life."

"Let me explain it to you." My guide seemed to conjure up energy forces all around us. "When you decide to have a life on earth, as you call it, what you do is draw to you the quantum energy that is the universe. You create out of this energy the atoms and molecules that make up your real world. You do this according to a pattern laid down by the greater consciousness of which you are only a part. You helped create the infant's body that you then think you occupy, and you live out the drama you call your life. You are pulled down into a gravitational field that you call Earth. Within this gravitational field the atoms and molecules you create are organized into seas and mountains, houses, buildings and other people's bodies. And on this stage set you construct the morality play that you think of as a lifetime."

"I see," I said. I wasn't sure that I saw, but it was gradually beginning to make sense to me.

As the words of my guide or mentor, another part of myself, echoed in my thoughts, I moved into the rapid-eye-movement state of sleep. Then I saw that I was joined in this place by the lady from the Christian Family Foundation.

She expressed some indignation at being in this strange location. She turned to my guide and then suddenly expressed a deep feeling of awe and delight. "Oh! You are Jesus! I feel the love coming from you. What a marvelous experience!"

The entity who was my guide smiled at her. "Yes, to you I am Jesus. You feel the love, the overwhelming hope, the sense of being safe in the Universe. But I am a portion of yourself also. The Jesus that you write about down on earth was asked if he were the Son of God. He responded, "God is within me, as He is within all of you. I am your personal Jesus, but I am also a higher part of yourself. To Dr. Wambach, here," he turned and gestured toward me, "I am another part of her consciousness because that's the way she perceives it. To you, I am the God of love, I am Jesus."

I turned and saw the gentleman from the Committee to Investigate Claims for the Paranormal. He seemed to resent having been lifted up out of his sleep and carried to this particular place. His thoughts went to the guide figure and he said, "Now exactly who are you? Are you somebody I'm hallucinating because of that Christian lady who was on the talk show tonight?"

"No, to you I am the insights that science has

brought. Now you will see me as the figure of Albert Einstein."

The scientist looked around. "What is that white light I see over there?"

"That white light, as you call it, is the border of your physical universe. I, Albert Einstein, tried to explain to you that the real world is just a world in which energy moves at the speed of light. When you enter the physical universe you experience light as you go down into the slower-moving particles that you call the real world. As your consciousness leaves the real world, at what you call 'death,' you see once more the white light which is the border of the physical universe. Once you move into the white light or beyond, you are back home in a world where energy moves faster than the speed of light. That's why we have no time, no space here. Time and space are relative," and the Einstein-guide figure smiled at the scientist. "That's called The Theory of Relativity."

The scientist nodded solemnly. "Now *that* I can understand."

I looked around and found the psychiatrist had joined us. He looked at the mentor and said, "Is this the great Dr. Freud?"

The guide smiled. "I am the Dr. Freud within you," he responded. "I know you've sought after knowledge through this life, but you've also chosen a path that involved you with the mundane affairs of mankind. You started out this lifetime as a psychiatrist with the hope of being able to bring some peace to people who are suffering. You feel as though you were side-tracked into serving a social world. Listen to me now. Seek into your own dreams, Psychiatrist, and find there a renewal of the purpose that you chose when you began this life."

The psychiatrist looked thoughtful. "Perhaps I don't

really have to change where I live in order to renew my life. Maybe what I need to do is to concentrate more intensely on the people who come to me for help, and through them I may find my purpose again."

Next to join us in this strange corner of the Universe beyond space and time was the gentleman from the Society for Ethical Hypnosis. "I don't know what I'm doing here," he fumed. "There's a great deal of real work to be done down in the world. I have a technique that I think can help people a great deal. I don't want to waste my time out here when there's so much to be done down there." The mentor turned to him.

"And who do you see me as?" he asked.

The hypnotist looked surprised. "Why, you look like my grandfather. In my very difficult childhood my grandfather was a great help to me. Even though I couldn't afford to go to medical school, my grandfather taught me the value of hard work and honesty. I've often felt him around me, though I know he was only in my mind. Am I just in my mind now? Is that why you are here, Grandfather?"

"Yes, you may see me as your dead grandfather encouraging you in the difficult challenges you set for yourself in this life. I'll be waiting here for you, and I'll see you not only in your dreams, but I'll see you when you finally leave the physical shell you call your body. You've done well so far in this life with a difficult set of circumstances, and I congratulate you."

The hypnotist looked pleased. "Well, I can't hang around here. I have to get up early because I have a long list of people to see today. Good-bye, Grandfather."

The hypnotist disappeared from my dream; the psychiatrist also was returning to his life on earth. The Christian lady was still wrapped in the warmth and happiness of the love experience she received from the mentor. I was alone once more with this other portion of myself.

Then I saw around me the floating figure of my subject who had been on the show with us. He smiled and waved gaily as he headed out for another part of the universe. He had his own places to explore, and he didn't need to stop with us here. He was following his own flight out into the stretches of the universe far beyond the white light.

My mentor turned to me. "It's time for your alarm clock to go off, too. It's time for you to go down back into your body and to wake up once more into that strange dream called being alive. You know that you've set yourself a lot of challenges, don't you?" he asked me.

"Yes. I know that a lot of people have been waiting for my research, and I know that controversy will surround it. Is it my challenge to be able to accept the criticism that will come?"

My mentor looked serious. "You know that the challenge is coming closer each moment. The challenge is not to be able to withstand criticisms, that's easy enough. The challenge is to be able to accept all of the ideas, the concepts, and the emotional feelings of all those around you. You can't associate with just those who believe as you do. I am within all of those people as I am a part of you. There is no isolation, no separateness, no you and me. Your challenge is to remember and accept this. Your challenge is to love everyone that you meet. Do you think that you can do that?"

"No, I don't think I'm up to that. I'm going to feel nasty, and mean, and I'm going to fight other people whose ideas I disagree with. But maybe you're right. If you stay with me, maybe I'll be able to rise above the arguments, and to see, love and understand all the people, all the thousands of people, that I will meet in the rest of my life."

"Well, all you can do is try. After all," and my guide smiled at me, "you may have to live many times before you finally learn this, the most important lesson. We are all one."

ABOUT THE AUTHOR

DR. HELEN WAMBACH is a psychologist who is fast becoming one of the most written and talked about women in America. Her book, *Recalling Past Lives: The Evidence From Hypnosis,* has recently appeared, and articles discussing her work have been published in such diverse publications as *Human Behavior, Time, California Living, Oui,* the *Village Voice* and the *Star.* Her article, "Life Before Life," (the basis for her book) was published in *Psychic Magazine* (Jan., Feb. 1977) and resulted in many letters and telephone calls from people throughout the United States who found her research absorbing and meaningful.

DON'T MISS
THESE CURRENT
Bantam Bestsellers

☐	23922	**GIRI** Marc Olden	$3.50
☐	23920	**VOICE OF THE HEART** Barbara Taylor Bradford	$4.50
☐	23638	**THE OTHER SIDE** Diana Henstell	$3.50
☐	23845	**THE DELTA STAR** Joseph Wambaugh	$3.95
☐	23709	**THE OMEGA DECEPTION** Charles Robertson	$3.50
☐	23577	**THE SEEDING** David Shobin	$2.95
☐	20476	**THE UNBORN** David Shobin	$2.95
☐	23198	**BLACK CHRISTMAS** Thomas Altman	$2.95
☐	22687	**TRUE BRIDE** Thomas Altman	$2.95
☐	24010	**KISS DADDY GOODBYE** Thomas Altman	$3.50
☐	23637	**THE THIRD WORLD WAR: THE UNTOLD STORY** Gen. Sir John Hackett	$3.95
☐	23481	**THE VALLEY OF HORSES** Jean M. Auel	$3.95
☐	23897	**CLAN OF THE CAVE BEAR** Jean M. Auel	$4.50
☐	23670	**WHAT ABOUT THE BABY?** Clare McNally	$2.95
☐	23302	**WORLDLY GOODS** Michael Korda	$3.95
☐	23105	**NO COMEBACKS** F. Forsyth	$3.95
☐	22838	**TRADITIONS** Alan Ebert w/ Janice Rotchstein	$3.95
☐	22866	**PACIFIC VORTEX** Clive Cussler	$3.95
☐	22520	**GHOST LIGHT** Clare McNally	$2.95
☐	23224	**A SEPARATE PEACE** John Knowles	$2.50
☐	20822	**THE GLITTER DOME** Joseph Wambaugh	$3.95

Prices and availability subject to change without notice.

Buy them at your local bookstore or use this handy coupon for ordering:

Bantam Books, Inc., Dept. FB, 414 East Golf Road, Des Plaines, Ill. 60016

Please send me the books I have checked above. I am enclosing $_____
(please add $1.25 to cover postage and handling). Send check or money order
—no cash or C.O.D.'s please.

Mr/Mrs/Miss_____

Address_____

City_____ State/Zip_____

FB—4/84
Please allow four to six weeks for delivery. This offer expires 10/84.

SPECIAL
MONEY SAVING
OFFER

Now you can have an up-to-date listing of Bantam's hundreds of titles plus take advantage of our unique and exciting bonus book offer. A special offer which gives you the opportunity to purchase a Bantam book for only 50¢. Here's how!

By ordering any five books at the regular price per order, you can also choose any other single book listed (up to a $4.95 value) for just 50¢. Some restrictions do apply, but for further details why not send for Bantam's listing of titles today!

Just send us your name and address plus 50¢ to defray the postage and handling costs.